Teacher Edition

Reveal MATH™
English Language Learner Guide
Course 3

Mc
Graw
Hill
Education

my.mheducation.com

Send all inquiries to:
McGraw-Hill Education
STEM Learning Solutions Center
8787 Orion Place
Columbus, OH 43240

ISBN: 978-0-07-697591-4 (Language Development Handbook, Course 3, Teacher Edition)
MHID: 0-07-697591-6 (Language Development Handbook, Course 3, Teacher Edition)
ISBN: 978-0-07-902926-3 (Language Development Handbook, Course 3, Student Edition)
MHID: 0-07-902926-4 (Language Development Handbook, Course 3, Student Edition)

Visual Kinesthetic Vocabulary® is a registered trademark of
Dinah-Might Adventures, LP.

1 2 3 4 5 6 7 8 9 10 LKV 27 26 25 24 23 22 21 20 19 18

Contents

McGraw-Hill Education's Guiding Principles for Supporting English Learners

McGraw-Hill Education is committed to providing English Learners appropriate support as they simultaneously learn content and language. As an organization, we recognize that the United States is a culturally and linguistically diverse country. Moreover, this diversity continues to increase, with corresponding growth in the number of English Learners (ELLs). In 2012–2013, an estimated 4.85 million ELLs were enrolled US schools; this subgroup now makes up nearly 10% of the total public school enrollment (Ruiz-Soto, Hooker, and Batalova, 2015). In fact, ELLs are the fastest growing student population in the country, growing 60% in the last decade, compared with only 7% growth of the general student population (Grantmakers for Education, 2013). Perhaps most interesting of all, the vast majority of ELLs – 85% of prekindergarten through fifth grade ELLs, and 62% of high school ELLs – were born in the United States (Zong & Batalova, 2015). These US-born ELLs may be first-, second-, or third-generation students with strong ties to their cultural roots.

A great many ELLs come to school with a variety of rich linguistic and cultural backgrounds from Spanish-speaking communities and countries all throughout the Americas. In addition to Spanish, there are some ELLs that come to school speaking fluent or limited Spanish in addition to an indigenous language native to North, Central and South America. In addition, schools experience native speakers from numerous other backgrounds and languages—the most common other languages being Cantonese, Hmong, Korean, Vietnamese, and Haitian Creole. While over 70% of ELLs come to school speaking Spanish as their native language, as a group, ELLs speak nearly 150 languages (Baird, 2015). The experiences and identities acquired in the context of ELLs' homes and communities can transform the simplest classroom into a unique cultural and linguistic microcosm.

English Learners' success in learning a second language is influenced by a variety of factors besides the instructional method itself, including individual, family, and classroom characteristics; school and community contexts; the attributes of the assessment used to measure progress; and whether the language acquired is a national or foreign language (August & Shanahan, 2006; Genesee, Lindholm-Leary, Saundes, & Christian, 2006). For instance, children's initial levels of proficiency in their home language(s), along with English, influence new language acquisition (August, Shanahan, Escamilla, K., 2009) as does the quality of school support (Niehaus & Adelson, 2014) and the characteristics of the language learners' first and second languages (Dressler & Kamil, 2006)

Given these factors, there is a pressing need for fundamental principles that guide the support of ELLs as they acquire content and develop language. Drawing upon extensive research in the field, McGraw-Hill Education has developed nine guiding principles for supporting English Learners at all grade levels and in all disciplines.

Guiding Principles

- ✔ Provide Specialized Instruction

- ✔ Cultivate Meaning

- ✔ Teach Structure and Form

- ✔ Develop Language in Context

- ✔ Scaffold to Support Access

- ✔ Foster Interaction

- ✔ Create Affirming Cultural Spaces

- ✔ Engage Home to Enrich Instruction

- ✔ Promote Multilingualism

Proficiency Level Descriptors

	Interpretive (Input)		Productive (Output)	
	Listening	**Reading**	**Writing**	**Speaking**
An Entering/Emerging Level ELL • New to this country; may have memorized some everyday phrases like, "Where is the bathroom", "My name is....", may also be in the "silent stage" where they listen to the language but are not comfortable speaking aloud • Struggles to understand simple conversations • Can follow simple classroom directions when overtly demonstrated by the instructor	• Listens actively yet struggles to understand simple conversations • Possibly understands "chunks" of language; may not be able to produce language verbally	• Reads familiar patterned text • Can transfer Spanish decoding somewhat easily to make basic reading in English seem somewhat fluent; comprehension is weak	• Writes labels and word lists, copies patterned sentences or sentence frames, one- or two-word responses	• Responds non-verbally by pointing, nodding, gesturing, drawing • May respond with yes/no, short phrases, or simple memorized sentences • Struggles with non-transferable pronunciations.
A Developing/Expanding Level ELL • Is dependent on prior knowledge, visual cues, topic familiarity, and pretaught math-related vocabulary • Solves word problems with significant support • May procedurally solve problems with a limited understanding of the math concept.	• Has ability to understand and distinguish simple details and concepts of familiar/ previously learned topics	• Recognizes obvious cognates • Pronounces most English words correctly, reading slowly and in short phrases • Still relies on visual cues and peer or teacher assistance	• Produces writing that consists of short, simple sentences loosely connected with limited use of cohesive devices • Uses undetailed descriptions with difficulty expressing abstract concepts	• Uses simple sentence structure and simple tenses • Prefers to speak in present tense.
A Bridging Level ELL • May struggle with conditional structure of word problems • Participates in social conversations needing very little contextual support • Can mentor other ELLs in collaborative activities.	• Usually understands longer, more elaborated directions, conversations, and discussions on familiar and some unfamiliar topics • May struggle with pronoun usage	• Reads with fluency, and is able to apply basic and higher-order comprehension skills when reading grade-appropriate text	• Is able to engage in writing assignments in content area instruction with scaffolded support • Has a grasp of basic verbs, tenses, grammar features, and sentence patterns	• Participates in most academic discussions on familiar topics, with some pauses to restate, repeat, or search for words and phrases to clarify meaning.

Collaborative Conversations

Students engage in whole-class, small-group, and partner discussions during every lesson. The chart below provides prompt frames and response frames that will help students at different language proficiency levels interact with each other in meaningful ways.

You may wish to post these frames in the classroom for student reference.

Core Skills	Prompt Frames	Response Frames
Elaborate and Ask Questions	Can you tell me more about it? Can you give me some details? Can you be more specific? What do you mean by...? How or why is it important?	I think it means that... In other words... It's important because... It's similar to when...
Support Ideas with Evidence	Can you give any examples from the text? What are some examples from other texts? What evidence do you see for that? How can you justify that idea? Can you show me where the text says that?	The text says that... An example from another text is... According to... Some evidence that supports that is...
Build On or Challenge Partner's Ideas	What do you think of the idea that...? Can we add to this idea? Do you agree? What are other ideas/points of view? What else do we need to think about? How does that connect to the idea...?	I would add that... I want to follow up on your idea... Another way to look at it is... What you said made me think of...
Paraphrase	What do we know so far? To recap, I think that... I'm not sure that was clear. How can we relate what I said to the topic/question?	So, you are saying that... Let me see if I understand you... Do you mean that...? In other words... It sounds like you are saying that...
Determine the Main Idea and Key Details	What have we discussed so far? How can we summarize what we have talked about? What can we agree upon? What are main points or ideas we can share? What relevant details support the main points or ideas? What key ideas can we take away?	We can say that... The main idea seems to be... As a result of this conversation, we think that we should... The evidence suggests that...

Strategies for Classroom Discussion

Providing multiple opportunities to speak in the classroom and welcoming all levels of participation will motivate English learners to take part in class discussions and build oral proficiency. These basic teaching strategies will encourage whole class and small group discussions for all language proficiency levels of English learners.

 Wait time/Different Response

- Be sure to give students enough time to answer the question. They may need more time to process their ideas.
- Let them know that they can respond in different ways depending on their levels of proficiency. Students can:
  - Answer in their native language; then you can rephrase in English
  - Ask a more proficient ELL speaker to repeat the answer in English
  - Answer with nonverbal cues.

 Elaborate

- If students give a one-word answer or a nonverbal clue, elaborate on the answer to model fluent speaking and grammatical patterns.
- Provide more examples or repeat the answer using proper academic language.

 Elicit

- Prompt students to give a more comprehensive response by asking additional questions or guiding them to get an answer, such as can you tell me more?
- This strategy is very effective when students are asked to justify or explain their reasoning.

 Asking about Meaning

- Repeating an answer offers an opportunity to clarify the meaning of a response.
- Repeating an answer allows you to model the proper form for a response. You can model how to answer in full sentences and use academic language.
- When you repeat the answer, correct any grammar or pronunciation errors.

ENTERING/EMERGING

- What is _____?
- What does _____ mean?
- _____ is _____.
- _____ means _____.

DEVELOPING/EXPANDING

- Could you tell me what _____ means?
- _____ is similar to _____.
- _____ is another way of saying _____.

BRIDGING

- Could you give me a definition of _____?
- Can you point to the evidence from the text?
- What is the best answer? Why?

✓ Talk about Level of Understanding

ENTERING/EMERGING	• I understand./I got it. • I don't understand this word/sentence.
DEVELOPING/EXPANDING	• Could you tell me what _____ means? • _____ is another way of saying _____.
BRIDGING	• I think I understand most of it. • I'm not sure I understand this completely.

✓ Justify Your Reasoning

ENTERING/EMERGING	• I think _____.
DEVELOPING/EXPANDING	• My reasons are _____.
BRIDGING	• I think _____ because _____.

✓ Agreeing with Someone's Reasoning

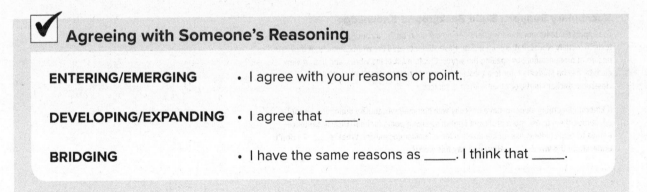

ENTERING/EMERGING	• I agree with your reasons or point.
DEVELOPING/EXPANDING	• I agree that _____.
BRIDGING	• I have the same reasons as _____. I think that _____.

✓ Disagreeing with Someone's Reasoning

ENTERING/EMERGING	• I don't agree with your reasons.
DEVELOPING/EXPANDING	• I don't agree that _____.
BRIDGING	• I can see your point. However, I think that _____.

How to Use the Teacher Edition

The suggested strategies, activities, and tips provide additional language and concept support to accelerate English learners' acquisition of academic English.

English Learner Instructional Strategy

Each English Learner Instructional Strategy can be utilized before or during regular class instruction.

Categories of the scaffolded support are:

- Vocabulary Support
- Language Structure Support
- Sensory Support
- Graphic Support
- Collaborative Support

The goal of the scaffolding strategies is to make each individual lesson more comprehensible for ELLs by providing visual, contextual and linguistic support to foster students' understanding of basic communication in an academic context.

Lesson 4 Dilations

English Learner Instructional Strategy

Vocabulary Support: Build Background Knowledge

To support students' vocabulary acquisition on a regular basis, encourage them to scan their texts to identify words that are unfamiliar. Have students read the words aloud or, if they are unsure of pronunciation, by spelling the words. Create a list of the words, and then review each by having students refer to a glossary, their math notebook, the Word Wall, the classroom anchor charts, or other reference sources.

If Entering/Emerging students have difficulty with non-math vocabulary during the lesson, encourage them to ask more proficient English-speaking peers for help. Display sentence frames to help students ask for clarification for unfamiliar vocabulary: **What is _____? I don't understand the word _____. How do I say this word?**

Since ELLs benefit from visual references to new vocabulary, many of the English Learner Instruction Strategies suggest putting vocabulary words on a Word Wall. Choose a location in your classroom for your Word Wall, and organize the words by module, by topic, or alphabetically.

English Language Development Leveled Activities

These activities are tiered for Entering/Emerging, Developing/Expanding, and Bridging leveled ELLs. Activity suggestions are specific to the content of the lesson. Some activities include instruction to support students with lesson specific vocabulary that they will need to understand the math content in English, while other activities teach the concept or skill using scaffolded approaches specific to ELLs. The activities are intended for small group instruction, and can be directed by the instructor, an aide, or a peer mentor.

English Language Development Leveled Activities

Entering/Emerging	Developing/Expanding	Bridging
Academic Vocabulary	**Word Knowledge**	**Act It Out**
Write and say *rational number*. Have students chorally repeat. Write *percent, decimal, whole number, mixed number*. Provide an example of each and then rewrite it as a rational number. For example, write $14\% = \frac{14}{100}$ and point to the fraction as you say, *rational number*. After providing examples for the other categories, write π. Point to the symbol as you say, *Not a rational number*. Provide more examples of writing numbers as rational numbers, including repeating decimals.	Create fraction cards so that there are enough for one per student pair. Include fractions that can be written as terminating decimals and others that cannot. Distribute one card to each student pair. Say, *Determine if the rational number on your card is a terminating decimal or a repeating decimal.* Give students a [ ] the answer. [ ] sentence [ ] use as they share their answers: **The repeating decimal is ____, so the rational number [is/is not] a terminating decimal.**	Divide students into small groups. Distribute a ruler and a small object (3 inches or smaller) to each group [ ] paper clips, [ ] of paper, buttons, and so on. Say, *Measure your object. Write the measurement as a fraction or mixed number, and then rewrite it as a decimal.* After completing the task, have students use the following sentence frames to describe their data: **The measurement is ____. ____ is a rational number because ____. ____ [is/is not] a terminating decimal because ____.**

Teacher talk is italicized.

Student talk is boldfaced.

Multicultural Teacher Tip

Sports are a common theme in real-world problems, but some sports played throughout the

Multicultural Teacher Tip

These tips provide insight on academic and cultural differences that you may encounter in your classroom. While math is the universal language, some ELLs may have been shown different methods to find the answer based on their native country, while their cultural customs may influence their learning styles and behavior in the classroom.

How to Use the Student Edition

Each student page provides ELL support for vocabulary, note taking, and writing skills. These pages can be used before, during, or after classroom instruction. A corresponding page with answers is found in the teacher resources.

Word Cards

Students define each vocabulary word or phrase and write a sentence using the term in context. Space is provided for Spanish speakers to write the definition in Spanish.

A blank word card template is provided for use with non-Spanish speaking ELLs.

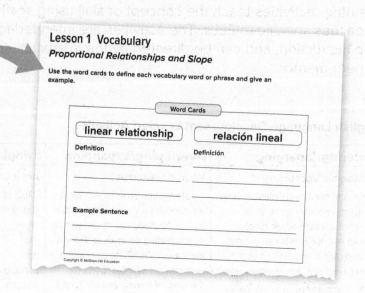

Lesson 1 Vocabulary
Proportional Relationships and Slope

Use the word cards to define each vocabulary word or phrase and give an example.

Word Cards

linear relationship   relación lineal

Definition   Definición

Example Sentence

Copyright © McGraw-Hill Education

Vocabulary Squares

Vocabulary squares reinforce the lesson vocabulary by having students write a definition, write a sentence using the vocabulary in context, and create an example of the vocabulary. Suggest that students use translation tools and write notes in English or in their native language on the cards as well for clarification of terms. Encourage students to identify and make note of cognates to help accelerate the acquisition of math concepts in English.

Lesson 2 Vocabulary
Angle Relationships and Triangles

Use the vocabulary squares to write a definition and a sentence. Then label the figure with an example for each vocabulary word.

| interior angle | Definition |
| | Sentence |

| exterior angle | Definition |
| | Sentence |

Three-Column Chart

Three-column charts concentrate on English/Spanish cognates. Students are given the word in English. Encourage students to use a glossary to find the word in Spanish and the definition in English. As an extension, have students identify and highlight other cognates which may be in the definitions.

A blank three-column chart template is provided for use with non-Spanish speaking ELLs.

Lesson 1 Vocabulary
Translations

Use the three-column chart to organize the vocabulary in this lesson. Write the word in Spanish. Then write the definition of each word.

English	Spanish	Definition
transformation		
preimage		
image		
translation		

Definition Map

The definition maps are designed to address a single vocabulary word, phrase, or concept. Students should define the word in the description box. Most definition maps will ask students to list characteristics and examples. Others, as shown at the left, will ask students to perform other tasks. Make sure you review with students the tasks required.

Lesson 1 Review Vocabulary
Solve Equations with Variables on Each Side

Use the definition map to list qualities about the vocabulary word or phrase.

Vocabulary

two-step equation

Characteristics

Description

Write three examples of two-step equations.

How to Use the Student Edition *continued*

Concept Web

Concept webs are designed to show relationships between concepts and to make connections. Encourage students to find examples or words they can use in the web.

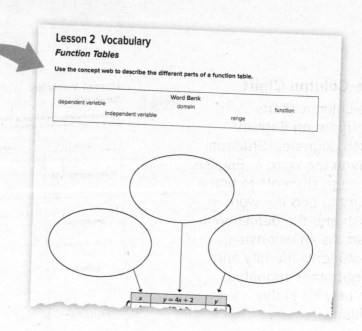

Lesson 2 Vocabulary
Function Tables

Use the concept web to describe the different parts of a function table.

Word Bank		
dependent variable	domain	function
independent variable		range

x	y = 4x + 2	y

Cornell Notes

Cornell notes provide students with a method to take notes thereby helping them with language structure. Scaffolded sentence frames are provided for students to fill-in important math vocabulary by identifying the correct word or phrase according to context.

Lesson 4 Notetaking
Estimate Irrational Numbers

Use Cornell notes to better understand the lesson's concepts. Complete each sentence by filling in the blanks with the correct word or phrase.

Questions	Notes
1. How do I estimate a square root?	First, I determine if the square root is a perfect _____. If not, then I use a _____ to determine between which two perfect _____ the square root falls and estimate based on where the square root falls on the number line.
2. How do I estimate a cube root?	First, I determine if the cube root is a perfect _____. If not, then I use a _____ to determine between which two perfect _____ the cube root falls and estimate based on where the cube root falls on the number line.

English\Spanish Cognates used in Course 3

English	Spanish	VKV Page Number
alternate exterior angles	ángulos alternos exteriores	
alternate interior angles	ángulos alternos interiores	
base	base	VKV45
bivariate data	datos bivariados	VKV80
center of rotation	centro de rotación	VKV29
coefficient	coeficiente	VKV7
composition of transformations	composición de transformaciones	
cone	cono	VKV45
congruent	congruente	VKV?
constant of proportionality	constante de proporcionalidad	
constant of variation	constante de variación	
corresponding angles	ángulos correspondientes	
corresponding parts	partes correspondientes	VKV71
cylinder	cilindro	VKV29
dependent variable	variable dependiente	
direct variation	variación directa	
equation	ecuación	
exponent	exponente	VKV?
exterior angle	ángulo exterior	
function	función	
function table	tabla de funciones	
hemisphere	hemisferio	VKV3?
hypotenuse	hipotenusa	VKV18
identity	identidad	VKV?
image	imagen	
interior angles	ángulos interiores	
irrational number	número irracional	VKV7
line of reflection	línea de reflexión	VKV?
linear equation	ecuación lineal	
linear function	función lineal	VKV38
linear relationship	relación lineal	VKV49

English/Spanish Cognates used in Course 3

English	Spanish	VKV Page Number
alternate exterior angles	ángulos alternos externos	
alternate interior angles	ángulos alternos internos	
base	base	VKV4
bivariate data	datos bivariantes	VKV39
center of rotation	centro de rotación	VKV29
coefficient	coeficiente	VKV7
composition of transformations	composición de transformaciones	
cone	cono	VKV33
congruent	congruente	VKV25
constant of proportionality	constante de proporcionalidad	
constant of variation	constante de variación	
corresponding angles	ángulos correspondientes	
corresponding parts	partes correspondientes	VKV31
cylinder	cilindro	VKV33
dependent variable	variable dependiente	
direct variation	variación directa	
equation	ecuación	
exponent	exponente	VKV4
exterior angles	ángulo externo	
function	función	
function table	tabla de funciones	
hemisphere	hemisferio	VKV35
hypotenuse	hipotenusa	VKV19
identity	identidad	VKV7
image	imagen	
interior angles	ángulos internos	
irrational number	número irracional	VKV3
line of reflection	linea de reflexión	VKV27
linear equation	ecuación lineal	
linear function	función lineal	VKV18
linear relationship	relación lineal	VKV9

English	Spanish	VKV Page Number
monomial	monomio	
multiplicative inverse	inversos multiplicativo	VKV7
nonlinear function	función no lineal	VKV17
perfect cube	cubo perfecto	VKV5
preimage	preimagen	VKV25
prism	prisma	
properties	propiedades	
Pythagorean Theorem	Teorema de Pitágoras	VKV21
qualitative graph	gráfica cualitativa	VKV15
radical sign	signo radical	VKV5
range	rango	VKV11
rational number	número racional	VKV4
real numbers	número reales	
reflection	reflexión	
regular polygon	polígono regular	VKV23
relation	relación	VKV13
relative frequency	frecuencia relativa	VKV37
rotation	rotación	
scale factor	factor de escala	VKV31
scientific notation	notación científica	VKV5
similar	similar	
sphere	esfera	VKV35
substitution	sustitución	VKV11
symmetric	simétrico	VKV37
systems of equations	systemas de ecuaciones	VKV11
theorem	teorema	
transformation	transformación	VKV27
translation	traslación	VKV25
transversal	transversal	
triangle	triángulo	VKV23
volume	volumen	
y-intercept	intersección y	

Lesson _____

Use the word cards to define each vocabulary word or phrase and give an example.

Word Cards

Definition

_____   _____

_____   _____

_____   _____

Example Sentence

_____

_____

- -

Word Cards

Definition

_____   _____

_____   _____

_____   _____

Example Sentence

_____

_____

Lesson _____

Use the three-column chart to organize the vocabulary in this lesson.

English	Native Language	Definition

Lesson 1 Powers and Exponents
English Learner Instructional Strategy

Language Structure Support: Tiered Questions

Add *base* and *exponent* and their Spanish cognates, *base* and *exponente,* on a Word Wall with examples or drawings to support understanding. Provide an exponent and have students recall what they learned in previous grades.

During the lesson, be sure to ask questions according to each student's level of English comprehension. Ask emerging level students simple questions that elicit one-word answers or allow the student to respond with a gesture: *Which number is the power? Is this the base?* or *Do I use _____ as a factor _____ times or _____ times?* For expanding students, ask questions that elicit answers in the form of simple phrases or short sentences: *How do I know which number to multiply? What do I need to do first?* or *Which numbers are the exponents?* For bridging students, ask questions that require more complex answers: *Why is _____ used as a factor _____ times?*

English Language Development Leveled Activities

Entering/Emerging	Developing/Expanding	Bridging
Academic Vocabulary Guide students to create a classroom anchor chart with visual examples and labels for *power, base,* and *exponent.* As you provide an example for each word and identify it, have students chorally repeat the vocabulary word. Monitor correct pronunciation and repeat the modeling as needed. In particular, listen to how students are saying *power,* as the /ow/ sound is not used in Spanish and may give students difficulty.	**Act It Out** Divide students into small groups of three or four. Distribute a pair of number cubes to each group. Say, *Roll your number cubes to create a power. Use the greater number as the base and the lesser number as the exponent. Write the power and find its product.* Give students time to complete the task. Then have the students in each group take turns describing the power using the following sentence frames: **The base is _____. The exponent is _____. The power is _____. The product of the power is _____.**	**Developing Oral Language** Have students work in pairs to create a three-column graphic organizer for the words *power, base,* and *exponent.* The left column should list the words, the middle column should contain an everyday definition for each word, and the right column should contain the mathematical definition for each word from the glossary. Afterward, discuss as a group how the everyday definitions for each word relate to the mathematical definitions.

Teacher Notes:

NAME _____ DATE _____ PERIOD _____

Lesson 1 Vocabulary
Powers and Exponents

Use the word bank to identify the parts of the expression. Draw an arrow from the word to the part of the expression it describes. Then use the three-column chart to organize the vocabulary. Write the word in Spanish. Then write the definition of each word. Sample answers are given.

Word Bank			
power	base	exponent	factor

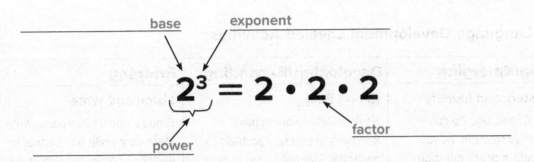

English	Spanish	Definition
power	potencia	product of repeated factors with an exponent and a base
base	base	in a power, the number that is the common factor
exponent	exponente	in a power, the number of times the base is used as a factor

Lesson 2 Multiply and Divide Monomials

English Learner Instructional Strategy

Graphic Support: K-W-L Chart

Write *monomial* and its Spanish cognate, *monomio*, on the Word Wall. Provide a concrete example by writing $3 \cdot 3 \cdot 3 \cdot 3 = 3^4$ or 81 and then identifying each monomial in the equation.

Display a K-W-L chart. In the first column, record what students learned in the previous lesson about powers. In the second column, record what students hope to learn during the lesson, including the use of the Laws of Exponents to simplify expressions that have multiple powers. After the lesson, display the following sentence frame and have students use it to describe what they learned during the lesson: **I learned that _____.** Use the third column of the K-W-L chart to record student responses.

English Language Development Leveled Activities

Entering/Emerging	Developing/Expanding	Bridging
Look, Listen, and Identify	**Report Back**	**Listen and Write**
Write $6^4 \cdot 6^2$ and say, *We can simplify this expression.* As you model simplifying, ask questions that students can answer as a group with thumbs up for **yes** or thumbs down for **no.** For example, point to the base of one power and ask, *Is this the exponent?* **no** Or ask, *Do I add the exponents?* **yes** Other questions you might ask are: *Do we add the bases? Do we multiply the exponents? Are the bases the same?* and so on. Repeat the activity by simplifying $\frac{8^5}{8^3}$.	Have students work in pairs. Randomly assign one problem to each pair. Give pairs time to work together to solve their assigned problems. Display the following sentence frames: **We were [multiplying/dividing] powers, so we [added/subtracted] the exponents. The expression _____ simplified is _____.** Have pairs use the sentence frames, share their answers, and describe how they simplified the expressions.	Group students into pairs. Write $x^4y^3z \cdot x^2z$ while one partner in each pair copies the expression on a sheet of paper. Addressing the other partners, say *Tell your partner how to simplify this expression.* Have these students explain each step as the students with the papers follow along to simplify the expression. Afterward, have pairs exchange papers to check each other's work. Write another expression with powers that can be simplified, and have the students switch roles as they repeat the activity.

Multicultural Teacher Tip

Students from some countries will not refer to *billion* as a place value until there are at least 13 digits. Instead, they refer to *thousand millions*, and *billion* is introduced when U.S. students would refer to *trillions*. For example, a U.S. student would read the number 564,321,000,000 as "five hundred sixty-four *billion*, three hundred twenty-one *million*," whereas a Latin American student would read it as "five hundred sixty-four *thousand*, three hundred twenty-one *million*."

NAME _____ DATE _____ PERIOD _____

Lesson 2 Vocabulary
Multiply and Divide Monomials

Use the definition map to list qualities about the vocabulary word or phrase. Sample answers are given.

Vocabulary

monomial

Characteristics:
What it is.

can be a number

Description

a number, variable, or product of a number and one or more variables

can be a variable

can be a product of a number and one or more variables

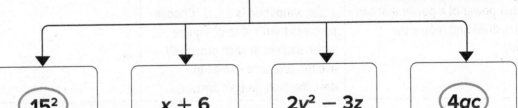

15^2 $x + 6$ $2y^2 - 3z$ $4ac$

Circle the expressions that are monomials

Lesson 3 Powers of Monomials
English Learner Instructional Strategy

Graphic Support: Venn Diagram

Display a Venn diagram. Label one side *Power of a Power* and the other side *Product of Powers*. Provide an example of each, such as $(6^4)^2$, $5^2 \cdot 5^3$, and a combination of the two $(6^4)^2 \cdot 6^8$. Then ask students to compare and contrast how each is simplified. Display the following sentence frames for students to use as they compare similarities and differences: **The bases are _____. The exponents are _____. When you simplify, you _____ the exponents.** Record student answers in the appropriate areas of the diagram.

As students work on practice problems, allow emerging students to partner with expanding or bridging students who share their native language. Have the emerging student participate in the discussion by suggesting answers to his or her partner using their native language. Then have the more proficient English speaker translate the answer to English.

English Language Development Leveled Activities

Entering/Emerging	Developing/Expanding	Bridging
Look, Listen, and Identify Write $(4z^4)^2$ and say, *We can simplify this expression.* As you model simplifying the expression, have students guide you by answering questions that can be answered with a single word. For example, point to the base and ask, *Do I add or multiply the exponents 4 and 2?* **multiply** Other questions you might ask are: *Will the base become 8 or 16?* **16** *Is z a base or an exponent?* **base** Provide another power of a power that can be simplified and repeat the activity.	**Numbered Heads Together** Have students get into groups of four. Ask the students in each group to number off as 1 – 4. Have the students in each group work together to find the volume of a cube with a side length of $3w^4$. Display the following sentence frames: **The formula for the volume of a cube is _____. The length of one side is _____. The expression _____ can be used to find the volume. The expression _____ simplified is _____.** Choose numbers from 1–4 to designate which student in each group will use the sentence frames to describe their group's answer.	**Building Oral Language** Have students get into six groups, and then assign one problem to each group. Say, *First, write the expression, then simplify the expression, and last, write out the expression in standard form.* Give groups time to complete the task. Afterward, compare the three versions and discuss why it is beneficial to have more than one way to write an expression.

Teacher Notes:

NAME _____ DATE _____ PERIOD _____

Lesson 3 Notetaking
Powers of Monomials

Use Cornell notes to better understand the lesson's concepts. Complete each
sentence by filling in the blanks with the correct word or phrase.

Questions	Notes
1. How do I find the power of a power?	I can _____multiply_____ the _____exponents_____ .
2. How do I find the power of a product?	I can find the _____power_____ of each _____factor_____ and _____multiply_____ .

Summary

How does the Product of Powers law apply to finding the power of a power?

See students' work.

_____

_____

_____

_____

_____

Lesson 4 Zero and Negative Exponents
English Learner Instructional Strategy

Vocabulary Support: Utilize Resources

As students review and utilize previously-taught vocabulary, such as *numerator, denominator, exponents,* and *powers of ten,* be sure to remind them that they can refer to a glossary or dictionary for help. Direct students to other translation tools as well if they are having difficulty with non-math language in the word problems.

Pair emerging level students with more proficient English speakers. Display the following sentence frames: **If the exponent is zero and the base is not zero, then _____. If the exponent is positive, then _____. If the exponent is negative, then _____.** Say, *Use the sentence frames to write three rules about powers.* Have the students in each pair complete the sentence frames. Then have the pair share what they have written.

English Language Development Leveled Activities

Entering/Emerging	Developing/Expanding	Bridging
Word Recognition	**Think-Pair-Share**	**Report Back**
Before the lesson, create a set of index cards with *add, subtract, multiply,* and *divide* written on them. Randomly distribute the cards so each student has one. As you work through problems from the lesson, have students guide you by prompting them with either/or questions for each step, such as *Do I add or subtract these numbers?* or *Do I multiply the exponents or add them?* Have students with the correct cards hold them up, and then choose one of these students to come forward and complete that step with you.	Before the lesson, use index cards to create matching pairs of expressions with positive and negative exponents, such as $10^3 \cdot 10^{-6}$ and $\frac{1}{10^3}$ or $y^{-2} \cdot y^{-3}$ and $\frac{1}{y^5}$. Distribute one card to each student. Say, *Find the student with a card showing an equivalent expression.* Give students time to find their partners. Then say, *Explain why the expressions are equivalent.* Display the following sentence frame for students to use when sharing their explanations: **_____ and _____ are equivalent because _____.**	Assign a problem to each student. Say, *Rewrite the problem using multiplication or division, and then simplify the expression.* Give students time to complete the task. Then display the following sentence frames for students to use in reporting back on how they arrived at an answer: **I rewrote _____ as _____. I [added/subtracted] the exponents. I simplified _____ to _____.** Have students evaluate each others' work and make suggestions when an incorrect answer is shared.

Multicultural Teacher Tip

In Mexico and Latin American countries, negative numbers can be represented two different ways: with either a negative sign in front of the number (i.e. −3) or with a horizontal line directly above the number (i.e. $\overline{3}$). The latter approach may be confusing, as it is also the common format for representing repeating decimals.

NAME _____ DATE _____ PERIOD _____

Lesson 4 Review Vocabulary
Zero and Negative Exponents

Use the definition map to list qualities about the vocabulary word or
phrase. Sample answers are given.

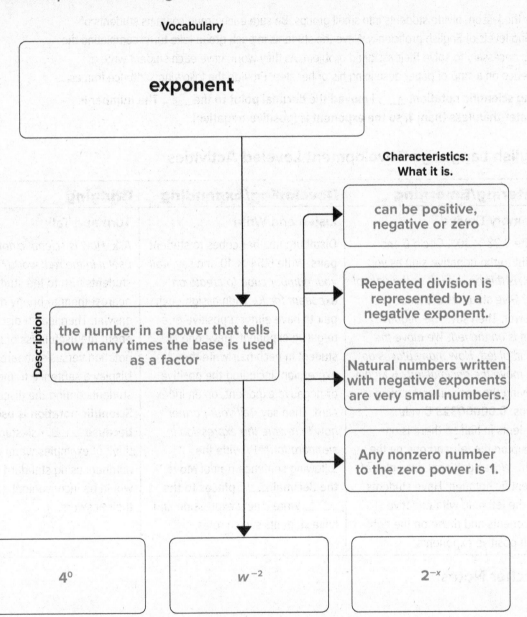

Vocabulary

exponent

Characteristics:
What it is.

can be positive,
negative or zero

Repeated division is
represented by a
negative exponent.

Natural numbers written
with negative exponents
are very small numbers.

Any nonzero number
to the zero power is 1.

Description

the number in a power that tells
how many times the base is used
as a factor

4^0

w^{-2}

2^{-x}

Write examples of terms that contain a negative or zero exponent.

Lesson 5 Scientific Notation

English Learner Instructional Strategy

Collaborative Support: Pass the Pen

Write the word *scientific notation* and its Spanish cognate, *notación científica,* on the Word Wall. Provide a concrete example by displaying a science text or other resource that includes numbers written using scientific notation.

After the lesson, divide students into small groups. Be sure each group contains students of varying levels of English proficiency. Have the students in each group take turns completing the steps necessary to solve their assigned problem. As they work, have each student write a sentence on a strip of paper describing his or her step. Provide the following sentence frames:

Using scientific notation, ____. I moved the decimal point to the ____. The number is [greater than/less than] 1, so the exponent is [positive/negative].

English Language Development Leveled Activities

Entering/Emerging	Developing/Expanding	Bridging
Memory Device	**Listen and Write**	**Turn and Talk**
Write 3.23×10^{-6}. Circle *6* and point to the negative sign as you ask, *Is this on the left or the right of six?* Give students a chance to answer. Then say, *The negative sign is on the left. We move the decimal left. How many places do we move the decimal left?* **6** Model moving the decimal and adding zeros. **0.00000323** Divide students in half so there is one group on the left and one on the right. Write additional examples of scientific notation. Have students on the left help with negative exponents and those on the right with positive exponents.	Distribute number cubes to student pairs. Write 6.54×10 and say, *Roll your number cube to create an exponent for 10.* Then assign each pair to have either a positive or a negative exponent. Have one student in each pair write the expression, including the positive or negative exponent, on an index card. Then say, *Tell your partner how to rewrite the expression in standard form.* Provide the following sentence frame: **Move the decimal ____ places to the ____.** Write a new expression and have students switch roles.	Ask, *How is scientific notation useful in the real world?* Have students turn to the student nearest them to briefly discuss the answer. Then lead a discussion about the usefulness of scientific notation versus standard form. Display a sentence frame to help students during the discussion: **Scientific notation is useful because ____.** Ask students to think of examples when writing numbers using standard form would be inconvenient and record their answers.

Teacher Notes:

NAME _____ DATE _____ PERIOD _____

Lesson 5 Vocabulary
Scientific Notation

Use the vocabulary squares to write a definition, a sentence, and a description
for each vocabulary word. Sample answers are given.

powers of 10	Definition
	ten raised to any power
Example	**When would you use this?**
10^2, 10^{-5}, 10^1, 10^{-3}	when using scientific notation

standard form of a number	Definition
	the usual way of writing a number that shows place values
Example	**When would you use this?**
25,000	writing numbers in everyday life

scientific notation	Definition
	a compact way of writing numbers with absolute values that are very large or very small
Example	**When would you use this?**
2.5×10^4	in a science experiment

Course 3 · Module 1 *Exponents and Scientific Notation* **5**

Lesson 6 Compute with Scientific Notation

English Learner Instructional Strategy

Language Structure Support: Sentence Frames

During the lesson, provide sentence frames such as the following to aid students in participating in the practice exercises:

Emerging: **Move the decimal _____ places. The power of ten is _____.**

Expanding: **Move the decimal _____ places to the _____. The exponent changes to _____.**

Bridging: **_____ must be rewritten as _____ because _____. The decimal must be moved _____ because _____.**

Have students work in small groups. Assign one problem to each group that they will solve together. Afterward, have a volunteer use the sentence frames to report back on how his or her group found the answer.

English Language Development Leveled Activities

Use the following problem with these leveled activities: *Evaluate each expression. Express the result in scientific notation.* $(3.9 \times 10^2)(2.3 \times 10^6) = $ _____

Entering/Emerging	Developing/Expanding	Bridging
Word Knowledge Invite four students forward and assign them as *first, second, third,* and *fourth.* Write the problem on the board and then, to the right, write *First.* Say, *First we need to multiply the decimal numbers.* Say, *first* again, have students repeat chorally. Then have the student assigned as *first* perform the task. Then write *Second* and repeat the activity for the next step. Continue in this manner for steps three and four. Choose a new problem and repeat the activity with four new students.	**Building Oral Language** Divide students into several small groups to symplify the problem. Display the following sentence frames: **First _____. Next _____. Then _____. Last _____.** Say, *Use the sentence frames to record each step as you symplify.* Give groups time to simplify the problem. Then ask a volunteer from each group to read the steps they took to simplify the problem.	**Exploring Language Structures** As you model simplifying the problem, write out each step using complete sentences, such as *1. I rewrite _____ as _____.* *2. I multiply _____ and _____.* and so on. Afterward, write another nearly identical problem for students to simplify on their own. Then say, *Use the sentences I've written to describe how you simplified the problem, but use the past-tense.* Listen for correct usage of the past tense and remodel as necessary.

Teacher Notes:

NAME _____ DATE _____ PERIOD _____

Lesson 6 Notetaking
Compute with Scientific Notation

Use Cornell notes to better understand the lesson's concepts. Complete each sentence by filling in the blanks with the correct word or phrase.

Questions	Notes
1. How do I multiply and divide with scientific notation?	I can _____multiply_____ the _____factors_____ and use the Product of Powers to _____add_____ the _____exponents_____. I can _____divide_____ the _____factors_____ and use the Quotient of Powers to _____subtract_____ the _____exponents_____.
2. How do I add and subtract with scientific notation?	First, I line up the _____place values_____ and rewrite each expression with the same power of _____10_____. Then, I use the Distributive Property and add or subtract the _____factors_____. Finally, I _____rewrite_____ in scientific form.

Summary

How does scientific notation make it easier to perform computations with very large or very small numbers? **See students' work.**

_____

_____

_____

_____

_____

_____

6 **Course 3 · Module 1** *Exponents and Scientific Notation*

Lesson 1 Terminating and Repeating Decimals

English Learner Instructional Strategy

Collaborative Support: Small Groups

Before the lesson add *rational number* and *decimal* and their Spanish cognates, *número racional* and *decimal,* on a Word Wall with examples or drawings to support understanding. Frequently refer to them to reinforce meaning and provide concrete examples of each word.

Divide students into four groups of varying levels of English proficiency. Have the students in each group work together to simplifying or converting some example problems. Then ask volunteers to take turns explaining the steps taken to get an answer. Display the following sentence frames to help them:

First we wrote the ratio as the fraction _____. Then we divided the numerator and the denominator by _____. The ratio in simplest form is _____. To find the decimal, we divided _____.

English Language Development Leveled Activities

Entering/Emerging	Developing/Expanding	Bridging
Academic Vocabulary	Word Knowledge	Act It Out
Write and say *rational number.* Have students chorally repeat. Write *percent, decimal, whole number, mixed number.* Provide an example of each and then rewrite it as a rational number. For example, write $14\% = \frac{14}{100}$ and point to the fraction as you say, *rational number.* After providing examples for the other categories, write π. Point to the symbol as you say, *Not a rational number.* Provide more examples of writing numbers as rational numbers, including repeating decimals.	Create fraction cards so that there are enough for one per student pair. Include fractions that can be written as terminating decimals and others that cannot. Distribute one card to each student pair. Say, *Determine if the rational number on your card is a terminating decimal or a repeating decimal.* Give students a few minutes to find the answer. Display the following sentence frame for pairs to use as they share their answers: **The repeating decimal is _____, so the rational number [is/is not] a terminating decimal.**	Divide students into small groups. Distribute a ruler and a small objects (3 inches or smaller) to each group. Objects may include paper clips, erasers, strips of paper, buttons, and so on. Say, *Measure your object. Write the measurement as a fraction or mixed number, and then rewrite it as a decimal.* After completing the task, have students use the following sentence frames to describe their data: **The measurement is _____. _____ is a rational number because _____. _____ [is/is not] a terminating decimal because _____.**

Multicultural Teacher Tip

Sports are a common theme in real-world problems, but some sports played throughout the U.S. may be unfamiliar to some ELLs. While soccer is played throughout the world, most countries refer to it as "football". For this reason, you may need to distinguish between "American-style" football and soccer and explain terms such as *touchdown* or *field goal.*

NAME _____ DATE _____ PERIOD _____

Lesson 1 Vocabulary
Terminating and Repeating Decimals

Use the vocabulary squares to write a definition, a sentence, and an example for each vocabulary word. Sample answers are given.

rational number	**Definition**
	the set of numbers that can be written in the form $\frac{a}{b}$, where a and b are integers and $b \neq 0$
Example	**Sentence**
$\frac{3}{5}$, 3, −5, −3$\frac{3}{5}$	All integers are rational numbers because they can be written with a denominator of 1.

repeating decimal	**Definition**
	the decimal form of a rational number
Example	**Sentence**
$0.\overline{3}$, 1.25000...., −0.1666...	A repeating decimal can have the repeating digit be zero.

terminating decimal	**Definition**
	a repeating decimal which has a repeating digit of 0
Example	**Sentence**
0.75, 1.25, −0.625	Fractions that have a denominator of 2 are terminating decimals.

Lesson 2 Roots

English Learner Instructional Strategy

Collaborative Support: Peers/Mentors

Write *radical sign* and its Spanish cognate, *signo radical*, on the Word Wall. Draw an example of a radical sign and use it as you discuss what students have learned in previous grades about squares and square roots.

Divide students into small groups with students of varying levels of English proficiency. As students work the first few problems, ask expanding or bridging students to answer first, and then encourage emerging students to repeat the answer in English. When emerging students are confident, invite them to be the first to answer their problems. Encourage them to use the sentence frame:

The square root of _____ is _____.

English Language Development Leveled Activities

Entering/Emerging	Developing/Expanding	Bridging
Multiple Word Meanings Draw a 5-by-5 array. Say, *This shows five times five or 25. What is the shape?* Give students a chance to answer, **square**. Then say, Yes. *It is a square. Five rows and five columns make 25.* Write $5 \cdot 5 = 25$ and $\sqrt{25} = 5$. Say, *Five squared is 25. So, five is the* **square root** *of 25.* Say, *square root* again as you point to the the square root symbol and have students repeat chorally.	**Frontload Academic Vocabulary** Divide students into five groups and assign each group one of the lesson vocabulary words: *square root, perfect square, cube root, perfect cube,* and *radical sign*. Have students list on an index card one or two everyday definitions for the individual words that make up each compound (*square, root, sign,* and so on). Have students flip the card over and write the math definition for each vocabulary word. Then have groups present both the math and non-math definitions and discuss how they are related.	**Developing Oral Language** Divide students into small groups and assign each group one of the following perfect squares: 9, 16, 25, 49, 64, 81. Say, *Write a real-world story problem that uses your assigned number and its square root.* If students need help getting started, you might suggest problems involving area or square arrays of seating, plantings, and so on. Give groups time to complete the task, and then have them present their story problems to the other students.

Teacher Notes:

NAME _____ DATE _____ PERIOD _____

Lesson 2 Vocabulary
Roots

Use the three-column chart to organize the vocabulary in this lesson. Write the word in Spanish. Then write the definition of each word. Sample answers are given.

English	Spanish	Definition
square root	raíz cuadrada	one of two equal factors multiplied to form perfect squares
perfect square	cuadrados perfectos	a rational number whose square root is a whole number
radical sign	signo radical	the symbol used to indicate a non-negative square root, $\sqrt{\ }$
cube root	raíz cúbica	one of three equal factors of a number
perfect cube	cubo perfectos	rational number whose cube root is a whole number

Lesson 3 Real Numbers

English Learner Instructional Strategy

Vocabulary Support: Cognates

Write *irrational number* and its Spanish cognate, *número irracional,* on the Word Wall with examples or drawings to support understanding. During the lesson, frequently refer to them to reinforce meaning and provide concrete examples of each word.

Write the prefix *ir-* and say, *This word part means "not." When it is added to the beginning of a word, it changes the word's meaning.* Remind students that *irrational* means "not rational," and then have them brainstorm other examples of words that use the *ir-* prefix, such as *irregular, irreversible, irresistible,* and *irresponsible.* Point out that *ir-* has the same meaning in English as in Spanish.

Refer students to a glossary or dictionary if they need a review of definitions for the different real number types: *natural numbers, whole numbers, integers,* and *rational numbers.*

English Language Development Leveled Activities

Entering/Emerging	Developing/Expanding	Bridging
Word Recognition Create a set of index cards so each student will have a card. On each card, write one of the following real number types: *natural, whole, integer, rational, irrational, real.* Distribute one card to each student. One at a time, display a wide variety of different number types and help students identify which number sets each falls into. For example, write 13.6 and say, *13.6 is a rational number. It is a real number.* Have students with either of those cards stand and say the word on their card. Be sure each number set is used multiple times.	**Partners Work** Write: *Order the set* { $\sqrt{5}$, 220%, 2.25, 2.$\overline{2}$} *from least to greatest.* Have students work in pairs to complete the exercise. Then discuss what steps had to be taken first before some numbers could be located on the number line. Display a sentence frame to help students: **First we had to _____.** Then have students identify which set or sets each number as originally written belongs to. Display another sentence frame to help students: _____ **is a** _____.	**Verbal/Linguistic Learners** Have students work in pairs. Provide each pair with a list of five number types: *natural, whole, integer, rational, irrational.* Tell students to take turns giving their partners numbers and asking the partner to categorize each number according to the list of number sets. The student who provides a number should then state whether he or she agrees or disagrees with the partner's categorization and why. Challenge students to find a wide enough variety of numbers so that all sets are included.

Multicultural Teacher Tip

ELLs who are familiar with the U.S. standard for placing the angle symbol at the front of a number or angle designation may be confused by the use of inequality symbols. They may have trouble distinguishing between the two signs, so it is important to emphasize the difference prior to beginning the lesson.

NAME _____ DATE _____ PERIOD _____

Lesson 3 Vocabulary
Real Numbers

Use the word cards to define each vocabulary word or phrase and give an example. Sample answers are given.

Word Cards

irrational number

Definition
a number that cannot be written
as the quotient $\frac{a}{b}$, where a and
b are integers and $b \neq 0$

Example Sentence
The square root of 2 is an irrational number.

números irracionales

Definición
número que no se puede
expresar como el cociente $\frac{a}{b}$,
donde a y b son enteros y $b \neq 0$

Word Cards

real numbers

Definition
the set of rational numbers
together with the set of
irrational numbers

Example Sentence
The set of real numbers include integers, fractions, mixed
numbers, percents, and irrational numbers.

número real

Definición
el conjunto de númerous
racionales junto con el conjunto
de númerous irracionales

Lesson 4 Estimate Irrational Numbers

English Learner Instructional Strategy

Language Structure Support: Choral Responses

As you work through the lesson and narrate the steps taken to estimate roots and cube roots, have students chorally repeat math words and phrases after you have said them. Prompt students by saying the math word or phrase a second time, emphasizing the correct pronunciation. Then have students chorally respond by repeating the word or phrase back to you. Listen closely for errors in pronunciation and model a second time if necessary.

Remember that some common sounds used in English may be unfamiliar to ELLs. For example, the /oo/ sound in *root* and the /kw/ sound in *square* are not used in some other languages. Students may also have difficulty with plurals, differentiating between /s/ at the end of *roots* and /z/ at the end of *squares* and *cubes*.

English Language Development Leveled Activities

Entering/Emerging	Developing/Expanding	Bridging
Listen and Identify	**Show What You Know**	**Round the Table**
List a few perfect and non-perfect squares. Point to each as you ask, *Perfect or not perfect?* Ask a volunteer to answer. Then say the answer: *perfect* or *not perfect*. Have students repeat chorally. Choose a non-perfect square and model estimating its square root by plotting it on a number line ranging between two perfect squares. Point to each end of the line as you ask, *Is the square root of _____ closer to _____ or _____?* Display the following sentence frame to help students answer: **The square root of _____ is closest to _____.** Repeat with a non-perfect cube.	Display a Word Web with *-er* written in the center and another one with *-est*. Have students brainstorm examples of comparatives and superlatives that use each ending and record them. Pair students and assign the following: $\sqrt{35}$ and $\sqrt[3]{62}$ to each pair. Display the following sentence frames to help them share their answers: **The greatest perfect square/cube less than _____ is _____. The least perfect square/cube greater than _____ is _____. _____ is closer to _____, so the best estimate is _____.**	Write: The number of swings back and forth of a pendulum of length *L* in inches per minute is $\frac{375}{\sqrt{L}}$. About how many swings will a 40-inch pendulum make each minute? Divide students into groups of three, and assign one problem to each group. Have students work jointly on the problem by passing the paper around the table to complete each step. Direct each member of the group to write with a different color to ensure all students participate. Afterward, have groups share their answers, and have the students in each group describe the specific steps they completed.

Teacher Notes:

NAME _____ DATE _____ PERIOD _____

Lesson 4 Notetaking
Estimate Irrational Numbers

Use Cornell notes to better understand the lesson's concepts. Complete each sentence by filling in the blanks with the correct word or phrase.

Questions	Notes
1. How do I estimate a square root?	First, I determine if the square root is a perfect ___square___ . If not, then I use a ___number line___ to determine between which two perfect ___squares___ the square root falls and estimate based on where the square root falls on the number line.
2. How do I estimate a cube root?	First, I determine if the cube root is a perfect ___cube___ . If not, then I use a ___number line___ to determine between which two perfect ___cubes___ the cube root falls and estimate based on where the cube root falls on the number line.

Summary

How can I estimate the square root of a non-perfect square? See students' work.

_____

_____

_____

_____

_____

_____

Lesson 5 Compare and Order Real Numbers
English Learner Instructional Strategy

Graphic Support: Number Lines

Review the vocabulary and language for the following types of numbers: *whole numbers, natural numbers, fractions, decimals, rational numbers, irrational numbers, real numbers integers*. Have students give examples of each type of number. Write their ideas on the board.

Draw a number line. Then tell students that they are going to put the example numbers in order on the number line. Ask, *How can we do this?* Students might say, **Compare numbers.** or **Find the smallest number first.** Suggest that students put all of the numbers in the same notation; for example, make all the numbers in decimal form, if possible. (Some numbers will have to be estimated.) Then have them put the numbers (estimates) on the number line.

Finally, have students use available language to compare two values at a time.

English Language Development Leveled Activities

Entering/Emerging	Developing/Expanding	Bridging
Choral Responses	**Sentence Frames**	**Communication Guides**
Have students compare two numbers on the number line. Say, *Point to the smaller number.* Students point. Model the sentence _____ **is the smaller number.** Have students repeat chorally. Then ask (about the same two numbers), *Is _____ greater than _____?* Model _____ *is greater than* _____. Have students repeat chorally. When students are firm as a group, have a few students say a sentence individually.	Assign a few numbers to each pair of students. Have them use any of the following sentence frames to compare the numbers and order them. _____ **is [greater/less] than** _____. _____ **is [bigger/smaller] than** _____. _____ **is the [greatest/least] number.** _____ **is [first/ second/ next/last/and so on] in order.**	Have partners repeat the Developing/Expanding activity. Then extend the activity to include more advanced language by using the following frames: _____ **is [greater/less/bigger/smaller] than** _____, **so it is [first/second/ next/ last/and so on] in order. Because** _____ **is [greater/less] than** _____, **it goes [first/second/...] in order. The [first/second/next/...] number is** _____ **because it is [greater/ less] than** _____.

Teacher Notes:

NAME _____ DATE _____ PERIOD _____

Lesson 5 Vocabulary
Compare and Order Real Numbers

Use the three-column chart to organize the vocabulary and key words in this
lesson. Write the word in Spanish. Then complete the definition of each word.

English	Spanish	Definition
repeating decimal	decimal periódico	Decimal form of a <u>rational</u> number
terminating decimal	decimal finito	A repeating decimal where the repeating digit is <u>zero</u>
square root	raíz cuadrada	One of the two <u>equal</u> factors of a number. If $a^2 = b$, then <u>a</u> is the square root of <u>b</u>.
rational number	número racional	A number that can be written as the <u>ratio</u> of two <u>integers</u> in which the denominator is not <u>zero</u>. All integers, fractions, mixed numbers, and percents are rational numbers.
irrational number	números irracionales	A number that cannot be expressed as the quotient $\frac{a}{b}$, where a and b are <u>integers</u> and $b \neq$ <u>0</u>.
real numbers	número reales	The set of <u>rational</u> numbers together with the set of <u>irrational</u> numbers.

Course 3 · Module 2 *Real Numbers* **11**

Lesson 1 Solve Equations with Variables on Each Side

English Learner Instructional Strategy

Collaborative Support: Show What You Know

Prepare a list of equations with variables on each side. Divide students into four groups of varying levels of English proficiency. Designate each group as one of the four Properties of Equality: *addition, subtraction, multiplication, division*. Then solve the equations. For each step, have a student from the appropriate group come forward and perform the step while explaining what he or she is doing: **I am _____ both sides of the equation.** Allow emerging students to just do the math or describe the step with a single word or short phrase, for example **dividing** or **adding** _____. Use each property a few times to ensure all students participate.

English Language Development Leveled Activities

Entering/Emerging	Developing/Expanding	Bridging
Building Oral Language Write $3x + 7 = x - 9$ on a large sheet of paper. Divide students into two groups. Give one group an algebra mat and algebra tiles. Give the other group the paper with the equation. Direct the first group to solve the equation for *x* using manipulatives. Display the following sentence frames: **Add _____. Subtract _____. Multiply by _____. Divide by _____.** As the first group completes each step using the tiles, have them guide the second group in solving the equation on paper. $x = -8$ Write a new equation and have groups switch roles.	**Exploring Language Structure** Assign a problem to student pairs. Have one student guide the other in solving the problem step-by-step. Display the following sentence frames: **Add _____. Subtract _____. Multiply by _____. Divide by _____.** Circulate and listen to students to be sure they are using the present tense. Then have the second student describe the steps they completed using the past tense. **I added _____. I subtracted _____. I multiplied by _____. I divided by _____.** Assign a different problem and have students switch roles.	**Partners Work** Divide students into pairs and distribute a number cube to each pair. Assign pairs as either *positive* or *negative*. Then say, *Roll the cube to determine a value for x. It will be positive or negative, depending on which you were assigned.* Direct students to write an equation with the variable *x* on both sides, based on their determined value of *x*. Have pairs trade equations and solve for *x*. Say, *As you solve, list each Property of Equality that you use.* Afterward, discuss which equations were more or less difficult to solve, and whether any did not work.

Multicultural Teacher Tip

Because many word problems involve money, ELLs need to understand American coins and bills. Display a chart that visually compares coin and bill values and models how to write dollars and cents in decimal form. You may also want to have ELLs describe the monetary systems of their native countries. Identifying similarities or differences can help familiarize students with the American system.

NAME _____ DATE _____ PERIOD _____

Lesson 1 Review Vocabulary

Solve Equations with Variables on Each Side

Use the definition map to list qualities about the vocabulary word or phrase.
Sample answers are given.

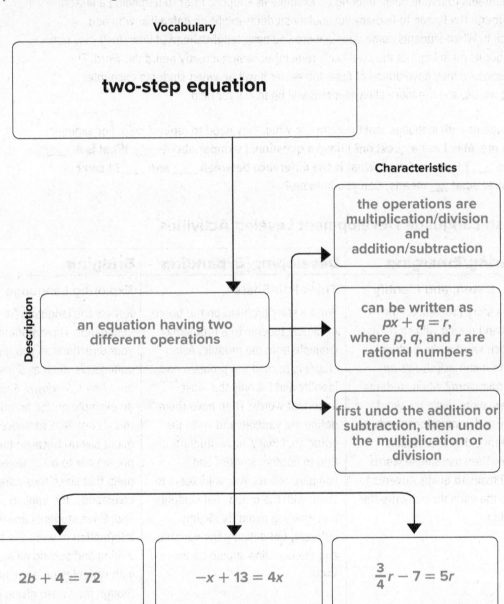

Vocabulary

two-step equation

Characteristics

the operations are multiplication/division and addition/subtraction

can be written as $px + q = r$, where p, q, and r are rational numbers

first undo the addition or subtraction, then undo the multiplication or division

Description

an equation having two different operations

$2b + 4 = 72$

$-x + 13 = 4x$

$\frac{3}{4}r - 7 = 5r$

Write three examples of two-step equations.

Lesson 2 Write and Solve Equations with Variables on Each Side

English Learner Instructional Strategy

Language Structure Support: Communication Guides

Review the terms *add, subtract, multiply, divide, equation, coefficient, constant,* and *variable.* Ask volunteers to define each, offering an example as support. Prior to beginning a lesson, scan through the lesson to find any vocabulary students might be unfamiliar with and preteach it. When students come upon a word you have taught ahead of time, they may not remember its meaning, but they will likely remember having already heard the word. The more exposure they have ahead of time, the easier it will be when students encounter difficult words, and the more likely students will be to ask for help.

Help students with language that they can use when they need to request help. For example, **Excuse me. May I ask a question? I have a question. I wonder about ____. What is a ____? Is this a ____? I am confused. What is the difference between ____ and ____? I can't remember what ___ means. Can you help me?**

English Language Development Leveled Activities

Entering/Emerging	Developing/Expanding	Bridging
Look, Listen, and Identify Write a story problem on the board and read it with students. For each word in the problem, point to it and ask, *Is this an important word?* When students say **yes,** write down the word. Then use the important words in a sentence that tells what is known. Then use simple words and phrases to guide students to define the variable and write the equation.	**Think-Pair-Share** Write a story problem on the board or direct students to a problem or example from the module. Ask students to read the problem and identify and list only the most important words. Then have them define the variable and write the equation. Finally, have students turn to another student and compare results. Ask volunteers to share with the group. Tell students that wording might be slightly different, but defining the variable and the equation should be the same.	**Exploring Language Structure** Review the language for commands. Have students follow your directions as you give commands, such as *Stand up. Raise your hand. Sit down. Smile.* Write an example on the board. Ask, *Is this a complete sentence?* Students might say **no** because there does not appear to be a subject. Tell them that since these are commands, the implied subject is *You.* Have students use this information to write the steps for writing and solving an equation with variables on each side as though they were giving commands to another person. Then have them say the commands to a partner who should follow them.

Teacher Notes:

NAME _____ DATE _____ PERIOD _____

Lesson 2 Review Vocabulary

Write and Solve Equations with Variables on Each Side

Use the vocabulary squares to write a definition, a sentence, and an example for each vocabulary word.

variable	**Definition** A letter or other symbol used to represent an unspecified number or value
Example Let p = cost of the peaches Let t = the cost of the tomatoes	**Sentence** Sammi defined the variables p and t to represent the costs of peaches and tomatoes.

expression	**Definition** a group of numbers, variables, and one or more operation that stands for the value of something
Example $5p + 2t$	**Sentence** Sammi wanted to buy five peaches and 2 tomatoes at the farmers' market and wrote an expression to represent it.

equation	**Definition** a mathematical sentence stating that two quantities are equal
Example $5p + 2t = c$	**Sentence** Sammi wrote an equation to calculate the total cost of buying peaches and tomatoes at the farmers' market.

Course 3 · Module 3 *Solve Equations with Variables on Each Side* **13**

Lesson 3 Solve Multi-Step Equations

English Learner Instructional Strategy

Vocabulary Support: Frontload Academic Vocabulary

During the lesson, have students work with a bilingual peer or mentor to solve the problems in the lesson. Before assigning the problems, define any unknown words using real-world objects, illustrations, and demonstrations to support understanding.

English Language Development Leveled Activities

Entering/Emerging	Developing/Expanding	Bridging
Word Identification	**Turn and Talk**	**Show What You Know**
Write the following equations on the board: $3(x - 10) - 6 = 11(x - 1) - 1$ and $15(c + 3) + 9 = 2(c + 1)$. Then write *factor, decimal, coefficient, rational coefficient, product, variable*. Have students copy each equation into their math notebooks. Then have them label each part of the equations using the terms on the board. After they have had time to work, ask volunteers to share answers. Model pronunciations as needed. In particular, help students note that the *ci* in *decimal* is pronounced /si/, the *cient* in *coefficient* is pronounced /shənt/, and the *-tion* in *rational* is pronounced /shən/.	Review these terms and their meanings: *Distributive Property, combine like terms, simplify, Properties of Equality*. Then write the following multi-step equation on the board: $3(x - 10) - 6 = 11(x - 1) - 1$. Have students first solve the equation independently. Then have them turn to a neighbor and explain their solution using this communication guide: **First, I used the ____ Property ____ and ____ by ____. Next, I ____. Then, I used the ____ Property. The solution is ____.**	Have students tell how solving multi-step operations is similar to solving one- or two-step equations. Then have them tell how it is different. Provide these sentence frames to help students form their responses: **Solving a two-step equation is [like/different from] solving a one-step operation because ____.**

Teacher Notes:

NAME _____ DATE _____ PERIOD _____

Lesson 3 Review Vocabulary
Solve Multi-Step Equations

Use the definition map to list qualities about the vocabulary word or phrase.
Sample answers are given.

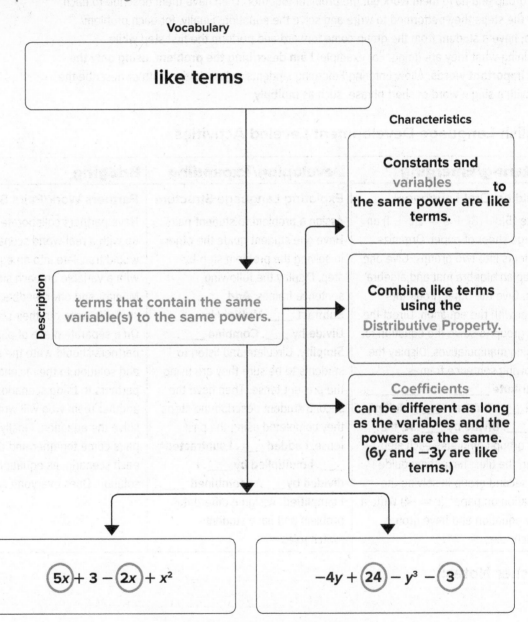

Vocabulary

like terms

Description

terms that contain the same variable(s) to the same powers.

Characteristics

Constants and __variables__ to the same power are like terms.

Combine like terms using the **Distributive Property.**

Coefficients can be different as long as the variables and the powers are the same. (6*y* and −3*y* are like terms.)

$5x + 3 - 2x + x^2$

$-4y + 24 - y^3 - 3$

Circle the like terms in each expression.

Lesson 4 Write and Solve Multi-Step Equations

English Learner Instructional Strategy

Collaborative Support: Show What You Know

Organize students into groups of varying levels of English proficiency. Assign a problem to each group and have them work out the problem together. Then have them describe to each other the steps they performed to write <u>and</u> solve the equation. Finally, for each problem/ group, have a student from the group come forward and perform the first step while explaining what they are doing. For example: **I am describing the problem, using only the most important words.** Allow Entering/Emerging students to just do the math or describe the step with a single word or short phrase, such as **multiply.**

English Language Development Leveled Activities

Entering/Emerging	Developing/Expanding	Bridging
Building Oral Language Write $15(c + 3) + 9 = 2(c + 1)$ on a large sheet of paper. Organize students into two groups. Give one group an algebra mat and algebra tiles. Give the other group the paper with the equation. Direct the first group to solve the equation for c using manipulatives. Display the following sentence frames: **Distribute _____ and _____. Add ____. Subtract ____. Multiply by ____. Divide by ____.** As the first group completes each step using the tiles, have them guide the second group in solving the equation on paper. ($c = -4$) Write a new equation and have groups switch roles.	**Exploring Language Structure** Assign a problem to student pairs. Have one student guide the other in solving the problem step-by-step. Display the following sentence frames: **Add ____. Subtract ____. Multiply by ____. Divide by ____. Combine ____. Simplify.** Circulate and listen to students to be sure they are using the present tense. Then have the second student describe the steps they completed using the past tense. **I added ____. I subtracted ____. I multiplied by ____. I divided by ____. I combined ____. I simplified.** Assign a different problem and have students switch roles.	**Partners Work/Pairs Share** Have partners collaborate to come up with a real-world scenario that would translate into an equation with a variable on each side. Monitor and offer feedback as students write out their scenarios. On a separate piece of paper, partners should write the equation and solution to their scenario. Ask partners to trade scenarios with another team who will write and solve the equation. Finally, have pairs come together and discuss each scenario, its equation, and the solution. Does everyone agree?

Teacher Notes:

NAME _____ DATE _____ PERIOD _____

Lesson 4 Vocabulary
Write and Solve Multi-Step Equations

Use the flow chart to review the process for writing multi-step equations. Then answer the questions at the bottom.

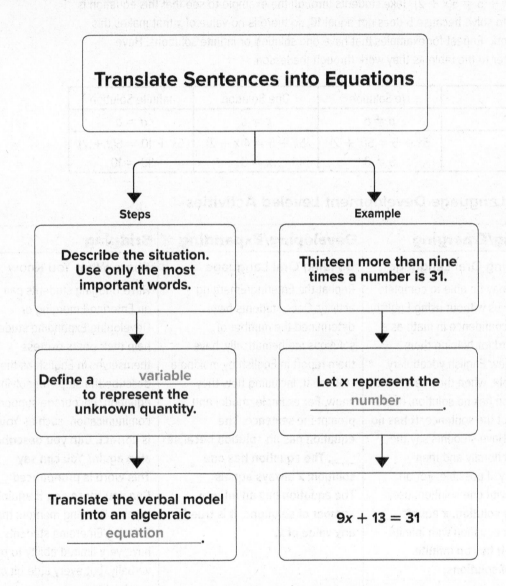

Translate Sentences into Equations

Steps

Describe the situation. Use only the most important words.

Define a ___variable___ to represent the unknown quantity.

Translate the verbal model into an algebraic ___equation___.

Example

Thirteen more than nine times a number is 31.

Let x represent the ___number___.

$9x + 13 = 31$

1. What are some key words that tell you to add? sum, total, more

2. What are some key words that tell you subtract? difference, less, decreased by

3. What are some key words that tell you to multiply? times, twice, area

4. What are some key words that tell you to divide? quotient, divided, half

Lesson 5 Determine the Number of Solutions
English Learner Instructional Strategy

Graphic Support: Graphic Organizer

Help students create a table that they can use for reference when determining the number of solutions to an equation. An equation will have no solution, one solution, or an infinite number of solutions. Show students an example of an equation that has no solution; for example, $5x + 5 = 5(x + 2)$. Take students through the example to see that this equation is impossible to solve because 5 does not equal 10, so there is no value of x that makes this equation work. Repeat for examples that have one solution or infinite solutions. Have students refer to the table as they work through the lesson.

	No Solution	One Solution	Infinite Solution
Symbols	$a \neq b$	$x = a$	$a = a$
Examples	$5x + 5 = 5(x + 2)$ $5 \neq 0$	$5x + 5 = 4(x + 2)$ $x = 3$	$5x + 10 = 5(x + 2)$ $10 = 10$

English Language Development Leveled Activities

Entering/Emerging	Developing/Expanding	Bridging
Developing Oral Language Students may be able to complete the problems without using English. Use their confidence in math as a springboard for helping them produce new English vocabulary. For example, when they determine an equation has no solution, model and prompt the sentence, **It has no solution.** Have students say the sentence chorally and then individually, if possible. For an equation with one solution, use, **It has one solution. x equals ___.** And for an equation with infinite solutions, **It has an infinite number of solutions.**	**Building Oral Language** Repeat the Entering/Emerging activity. Once students have determined the number of solutions mathematically, have them report in English by making a statement, including how they know. For example, model and prompt the sentence, **The equation has no solution because ___. The equation has one solution; x always equals ___. The equation has an infinite number of solutions; it is true for any value of x.**	**Share What You Know** Have Bridging students pair with an Entering/Emerging or Developing/Expanding student and help their peers express themselves in English as they describe the steps for solving an equation. Encourage supportive communication, such as **Your math is correct. Can you describe this step again? You can say ___. This word is pronounced ___. Can you try saying it again?** Remind Bridging mentors that Entering/Emerging students may have very limited ability to respond verbally, but every little bit of practice helps.

Teacher Notes:

NAME _____ DATE _____ PERIOD _____

Lesson 5 Review Vocabulary
Determine the Number of Solutions

Use the three-column chart to organize the vocabulary and key words in this lesson. Write the word in Spanish. Then write the definition of each word.

English	Spanish	Definition
coefficient	coeficiente	The numerical factor of a term that contains a ___variable___
constant	constante	A term without a ___variable___
equation	ecuación	A mathematical sentence stating that two quantities are ___equal___
solution	solución	Any value that satisfies an ___equation___
inverse operations	peraciones inversas	Pairs of operations that ___undo___ each other. For example, multiplication and ___division___ are inverse operations.

Lesson 1 Proportional Relationships and Slope

English Learner Instructional Strategy

Graphic Support: Word Webs

Write *linear relationship* and its Spanish cognate, *relación lineal,* on the Word Wall. Provide concrete examples by plotting a linear relationship on a graph.

Use a word web, and write *constant* in the center. Guide students in completing the web with synonyms for *constant* (*same, unchanging, steady*) and examples of constant events (sun rising, seasons, lunar cycles). Repeat for *change* and *rate.*

Display the following sentence frames to help students during the lesson:

The constant rate of change is _____ per _____.

The rate of change is not constant because _____.

English Language Development Leveled Activities

Entering/Emerging	Developing/Expanding	Bridging
Basic Vocabulary	**Academic Vocabulary**	**Act It Out**
Create two 2-by-5 tables. Label one table *Weeks* and *Days,* and the other *Months* and *Days.* Refer to a calendar as you read the days of the week and track the total with tally marks. Have students say the days along with you. Use the first table to show a constant rate of change for weeks (1:7; 2:14; etc.). Then start with the current month and say, _____ *days in* _____. Have students chorally repeat. Continue for five months. Record the data in the second table. Graph both tables to compare a constant rate of change with one that is not constant.	Divide students into two groups. Give one group color tiles and a ruler. Have them measure to the nearest $\frac{1}{4}$-inch as they add three tiles at a time, up to 15 tiles total. Give the other group paper clips and a ruler. Have them measure one paper clip, add two more and measure again, add three more, and so on five times. Have the groups record their data in a table and graph it. Afterward, have groups say whether the change was constant, whether it was a linear relationship, and whether the linear relationship was proportional.	Have pairs of students take turns performing a physical task, such as jumping jacks or sit-ups, for 5 minutes. The partner who is not performing the task will keep time and track the number of actions performed per minute. After each partner has completed the task, ask teams to organize their information in a table and determine the rate of change. Ask them whether the rate of change was constant or not. Have them use the rate to find the number of actions they would have performed in 5 minutes if their rate had remained constant.

Multicultural Teacher Tip

Word problems are an important part of the math curriculum, but they are especially challenging for ELLs. Allow students to share examples from their own cultures, including popular national sports, foods and drinks from their culture, traditional clothing worn in their home countries, and so on. When appropriate, help ELLs reword an exercise to include a familiar cultural reference.

NAME _____ DATE _____ PERIOD _____

Lesson 1 Vocabulary
Proportional Relationships and Slope

Use the word cards to define each vocabulary word or phrase and give an example. Sample answers are given.

Word Cards

linear relationship

Definition

a relationship that has a
straight-line graph

Example Sentence

A store sells sandwiches for $3 each. The relationship between
price and number of sandwiches is a linear relationship.

relación lineal

Definición

relación cuya gráfica es una
recta

Word Cards

constant rate of change

Definition

the rate of change between any two
points in a linear relationship is the
same or constant

Example Sentence

A store sells sandwiches for $3 each. There is a constant rate
of change between the price and number of sandwiches.

tasa constant de cambio

Definición

la tasa de cambio entre dos puntos
cualesquiera en una relación lineal
permanece igual o constante

Lesson 2 Slope of a Line
English Learner Instructional Strategy

Collaborative Support: Echo Reading

Pair Entering/Emerging students with Developing/Expanding or Bridging students. Write *rise, run,* and *slope.* Direct pairs to locate the terms in a glossary or math dictionary and copy the definition for each on a sheet of paper. Have the more proficient English speaker read aloud *rise* and its definition and pass the sheet to the other student. The Entering/Emerging student will read aloud *rise* and, if comfortable, the definition as well. Repeat for other words. Be sure students are differentiating between the /z/ sound in *rise* and the /s/ sound in *slope.*

Distribute paper and a ruler to each pair. Direct them to draw a diagonal line from a vertical side to a horizontal side, creating a right triangle. Say, *Measure the base and height to the nearest inch. Then determine the slope.* Display sentence frames for students to describe the slope:

The rise is _____. The run is _____. The slope is _____.

English Language Development Leveled Activities

Entering/Emerging	Developing/Expanding	Bridging
Frontload Academic Vocabulary Show an image of a sunrise. Point up as you say, *Sunrise. The sun comes up.* Then pretend to be sleeping and then waking. Say, *When I wake up, I rise.* Display a sloping line between two points on a graph. Then draw lines to indicate the rise and run. Draw an upward arrow next to the rise as you say, *Rise.* Have students chorally repeat. In a similar manner, demonstrate *run* by running back and forth before indicating the run on the graph and having students chorally repeat *run.* For *slope,* display an image of a ski slope.	**Report Back** Divide students into pairs. Distribute graph paper to each pair, along with two number cubes. In a hat or other container, place several scraps of paper with either + or − written on them. Say, *Roll your number cubes. Use one number as a rise and the other as a run.* Then have each pair draw a paper from the hat to determine the direction of their slope. Give students time to graph their lines. Then display the following sentence frames for students to report back: **The rise is _____. The run is _____. The slope is _____.**	**Share What You Know** Have students work in pairs. Give each pair a drinking straw and one-inch grid paper with an *x*- and *y*-axis drawn on it. Say, *Drop the straw on the graph paper. Draw a line that follows the straw. Make sure the line goes through two definite points.* Have students label the points, the rise, and the run. Then have students use the points to find the slope of the line. Ask, *If a younger student wanted to know how to find the slope of a line, how would you explain it?* Have volunteers share their answers.

Teacher Notes:

NAME _____ DATE _____ PERIOD _____

Lesson 2 Vocabulary
Slope of a Line

Use the concept web to define slope in five different ways.   Sample answers are given.

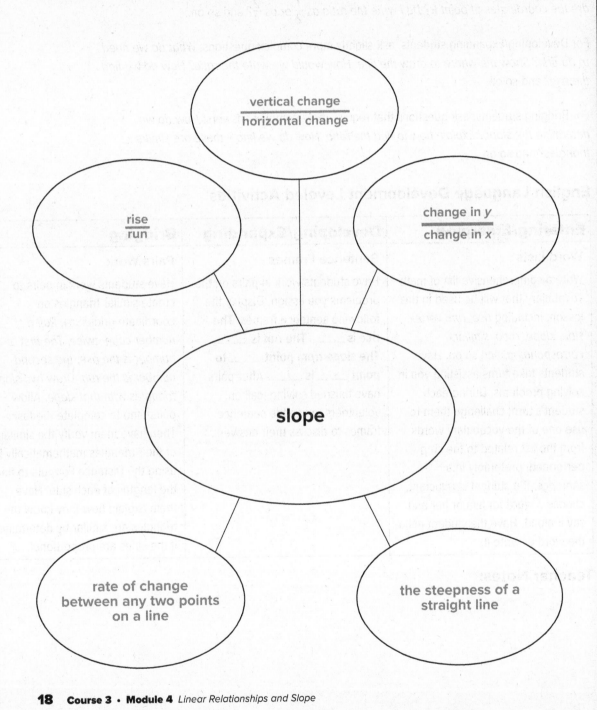

Lesson 3 Similar Triangles and Slope
English Learner Instructional Strategy

Language Structure Support: Tiered Questions

During the lesson, be sure to ask questions according to ELLs' level of English proficiency. Ask Entering/Emerging students simple questions that elicit one-word answers or allow the student to respond with a gesture: *Is this line the rise or the run? Show me the slope. What are the coordinates of point R? Do I write the ratio as $\frac{1}{2}$ or as $\frac{2}{1}$?* and so on.

For Developing/Expanding students, ask slightly more complex questions: *What do we need to do first? Show me where to draw the line. How would we write the ratio? How do we find the rise?* and so on.

For Bridging students, ask questions that require more complex answers: *How do we determine the slope? Explain how to find the ratio. How do we know these are similar triangles?* and so on.

English Language Development Leveled Activities

Entering/Emerging	Developing/Expanding	Bridging
Word Lists	**Sentence Frames**	**Pairs Work**
Write a comprehensive list of math vocabulary that will be used in this lesson, including *rise, run, vertex, side, slope, ratio, similar, corresponding,* and so on. Have students take turns assisting you in solving problems. During each student's turn, challenge them to use one of the vocabulary words from the list related to the step performed, preferably in a sentence. If a student is reluctant, choose a word for him or her and say it aloud. Have the student echo the word or write it.	Have students work in pairs on the problems you assign. Display the following sentence frames: **The rise is _____. The run is _____. The slope from point _____ to point _____ is _____.** After pairs have finished solving, call on volunteers to use the sentence frames to discuss their answers.	Have students work in pairs to create similar triangles on coordinate grids. Say, *Roll a number cube twice. The first number is the rise, the second number is the run. Draw two slope triangles with that slope.* Allow pairs time to complete the task. Then have them verify the similarity of their triangles mathematically by using the Distance Formula to find the lengths of each side. Have them explain how they know the triangles are similar by determining if the sides are proportional.

Teacher Notes:

NAME _____ DATE _____ PERIOD _____

Lesson 3 Review Vocabulary
Similar Triangles and Slope

Use the word cards to define each vocabulary word or phrase and give an example. **Sample answers are given.**

Word Cards

slope triangle	triángulo de pediente
Definition	**Definición**
Right triangles that fall on the same line on the coordinate plane.	Triángulos rectos que caen en la misma línea en el plano de coordenadas.
Example Sentence	
Slope triangles are similar, so their corresponding sides are proportional.	

Word Cards

similar figures	figures semejantes
Definition	**Definición**
Figures that have the same shape but not necessarily the same size.	Figuras que tienen la misma forma pero no necesariamente el mismo tamaño.
Example Sentence	
Similar figures have corresponding sides that are proportional and angles that are congruent.	

Lesson 4 Direct Variation

English Learner Instructional Strategy

Vocabulary Support: Utilize Resources

Write *direct variation, constant of variation,* and *constant of proportionality* and their Spanish cognates, *variación directa, constante de variación,* and *constante de proporcionalidad,* on the Word Wall and provide concrete examples for each word.

As students work through the lesson, be sure to remind them that they can refer to a glossary or multilingual dictionary for help, or direct students to other translation tools if they are having difficulty with non-math language in the problems, such as *earnings, travel, assume, repair, stain, deck,* and so on.

English Language Development Leveled Activities

Entering/Emerging	Developing/Expanding	Bridging
Non-Transferable Sounds	**Sentence Frames**	**Turn & Talk**
Guide students to create a classroom anchor chart with visual examples for *direct variation, constant of variation,* and *constant of proportionality.* As you provide examples, identify them by saying aloud the corresponding vocabulary phrase, and then have students chorally repeat. Monitor correct pronunciation and repeat the modeling as needed. In particular, listen for the /sh/ sound used in the suffix *-tion.* Native Spanish speakers may default to using the /s/ sound, as /sh/ is not used in Spanish.	Divide students into four groups. Randomly assign a problem to each group. After groups have finished solving, have them use the following sentence frames to share how they arrived at their answers: **First, I needed to know ____. I used the equation y = ____ to represent the ____. I divided ____ to find the value of ____.** Then ask, *What is the slope of your line? What does it tell you about the constant of variation?* After groups determine the slope, have them answer: **The slope is ____, so the constant of variation is also ____.**	Display the following sentence frame: **When a line passes through the origin, I know ____ because ____.** Then display a pair of coordinate planes: one with a line passing through the origin, and one with a line that does not pass through the origin. Ask, *Which of these graphs shows a direct variation? How do you know? Turn to your neighbor and discuss the answer.* Give students a moment to discuss the answer with another student. Then have volunteers use the sentence frame to answer.

Multicultural Teacher Tip

In some cultures, mental math is strongly emphasized. Latin American students in particular may skip intermediate steps when performing algorithms such as long division. Whereas U.S. students are taught to write the numbers they will be subtracting in the process of long division, Latin American students will make the calculations mentally and write only the results.

Lesson 4 Vocabulary

Direct Variation

Use the vocabulary squares to write a definition, a sentence, and an example for each vocabulary word. Sample answers are given.

direct variation	**Definition** the relationship between two variable quantities that have a constant ratio and whose graph passes through the origin
Example The store sells sandwiches for $3 each. The price varies directly with the number of sandwiches.	**Sentence** The relationship between the price of sandwiches and the number of $3 sandwiches is a direct variation.

constant of variation	**Definition** the constant ratio in a direct variation
Example In the direct variation equation $d = 3s$, 3 is the constant of variation.	**Sentence** The store sells sandwiches for $3 each. The constant of variation is 3.

constant of proportionality	**Definition** the constant ratio in a proportional linear relationship
Example In the equation $d = 3s$, 3 is the constant of proportionality.	**Sentence** The store sells sandwiches for $3 each. The constant of proportionality is 3.

Lesson 5 Slope-Intercept Form
English Learner Instructional Strategy

Graphic Support: Charts

Write *intercept* and its Spanish cognate, *interceptar,* on the Word Wall. Discuss math and non-math meanings of *intercept.* If students are familiar with *interception* as a football term, you might relate the sports meaning to the math meaning. Draw two points and connect them with a line. Say, *The quarterback is throwing the ball to the receiver.* Then add an *x*- and *y*-axis so the *y*-axis crosses the line. Say, *But the y-axis comes along and "intercepts" the ball. Where that happens is called the y-intercept.*

Draw a three-column chart labeled *First, Next, Last,* and display the following sentence frames: **The slope is _____. The *y*-intercept is _____. The equation is _____.** As applicable, have students use the sentence frames to describe how to solve a problem step-by-step. Record each step in the chart.

English Language Development Leveled Activities

Entering/Emerging	Developing/Expanding	Bridging
Look, Listen, and Identify	**Show What You Know**	**Academic Word Knowledge**
Write *slope* and *y-intercept,* say each term aloud as you point to it, and have students chorally repeat. Then have students line up. Write an equation in slope-intercept form below the two terms, point to part of the equation, and ask the first student in line, *Slope or y-intercept?* Have the student answer either verbally or by pointing to the correct term. Have the student write a new equation for the next student in line. After all students have had a turn, show graphs of linear equations and have students identify the *y*-intercepts.	Have students get into groups of four. Write then read aloud, *It costs $7 to get into an international food fair. At each booth, it costs an additional $3 to buy a plate of food. What is the total cost for attending the fair and sampling dishes from 4 booths?* Direct groups to write an equation for the cost of attending the fair and then graph it. $y = 3x + 7$ Display the following sentence frames to help students discuss their answers: **The equation is _____. The slope is _____. The *y*-intercept is _____. The total cost is _____.**	Divide students into four groups, and distribute three index cards to each group. Write *slope, y-intercept, slope-intercept form.* Say, *Work together in your groups to write a definition for each term on separate index cards.* Afterward, collect the cards. Display the definition found in a dictionary for each term. Randomly choose one of the groups' definitions and lead a discussion comparing it to the dictionary definition.

Teacher Notes:

NAME _____ DATE _____ PERIOD _____

Lesson 5 Vocabulary
Slope-Intercept Form

Use the concept web and the word bank to identify the parts of an equation in
slope-intercept form. Sample answers are given.

Word Bank			
slope	*x*-coordinate	*y*-coordinate	*y*-intercept

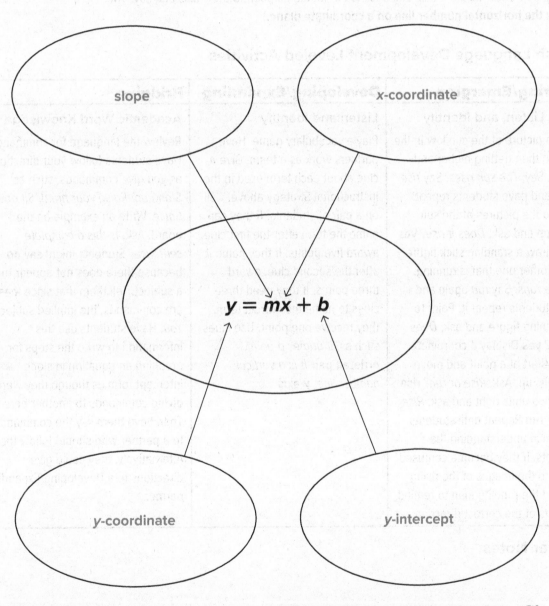

Lesson 6 Graph Linear Equations

English Learner Instructional Strategy

Language Structure Support: Tiered Questions

Before students begin the lesson and watch the lesson video for graphing, preteach or review the following terms: *graph, x-axis, y-axis, point, ordered pair, rise, run, slope, y-intercept, slope-intercept form, unit*. Display a graph and use it to review the terms. Check students' understanding by asking questions that are appropriate to each group.

For example:

Entering/Emerging: Point to the *x*-axis. Ask, *Is this the x-axis?* **yes**

Developing/Expanding: Point to the *x*-axis. Ask, *What is this?* **x-axis**

Bridging: Say, *Show us the x-axis and describe it.* (Students point to the *x*-axis and say, **The x-axis is the horizontal number line on a coordinate plane.**)

English Language Development Leveled Activities

Entering/Emerging	Developing/Expanding	Bridging
Look, Listen, and Identify Draw a picture of the sun low in the sky and then getting higher and higher. Say, *The sun rises*. Say *rise* again and have students repeat. Point to the pictures of the sun going up and ask, *Does it rise?* **yes** Next, draw a standing stick figure and another one that is running. Say, *He runs*. Say *run* again and have students repeat it. Point to the running figure and ask, *Does he run?* **yes** Display a coordinate plane. Start at a point and move two units up. Ask, *Rise or run?* **rise** Move two units right and ask, *Rise or run?* **run** Repeat until students are firm in understanding the concepts. If they become confused, return to the images of the rising sun and the running man to remind students of the correct direction.	**Listen and Identify** Play a vocabulary game. Have partners work as a team. Give a clue about each term used in the Instructional Strategy above. Call on a pair of students. If they can name the term after the first clue, award five points. If they name it after the second clue, award three points. If they need three clues to name the correct term, they receive one point. Use clues such as, *It names a point.* **ordered pair** *It is a vertical number line.* **y-axis**	**Academic Word Knowledge** Review the language for commands. Have students follow your directions as you give commands, such as *Stand up. Raise your hand. Sit down. Smile*. Write an example on the board. Ask, *Is this a complete sentence?* Students might say **no** because there does not appear to be a subject. Tell them that since these are commands, the implied subject is *You*. Have students use this information to write the steps for graphing an equation in slope-intercept form as though they were giving commands to another person. Then have them say the commands to a partner who should follow them. Alternatively, they could give directions to a Developing/Expanding partner.

Teacher Notes:

Lesson 6 Notetaking
Graph Linear Equations

Use Cornell notes to better understand the lesson's concepts. Complete each
sentence by filling in the blanks with the correct word or phrase.

Questions	Notes
1. What is the equation of a horizontal line? What does the graph of the line look like?	The equation of a horizontal line is y = b, where *b* is the value of the y-coordinates. A horizontal line is **(curved, straight)**, and parallel to the x-axis.
2. What is the equation of a vertical line? What does the graph of the line look like?	The equation of a vertical line is x = a, where *a* is the value of the x-coordinates. A vertical line goes straight up and ___down___ and is parallel to the y-axis.

Summary

How does the equation of a line written in slope-intercept form help you
graph the line?

See students' work.

_____

_____

_____

_____

_____

_____

_____

_____

_____

Lesson 1 Identify Functions

English Learner Instructional Strategy

Sensory Support: Function Machines and Tables

Use a box to create a "function machine." Write $x + 1$ on a card and use it to label the machine. Set a bucket of blocks labeled *input (x)* on one side of the machine. Set an empty bucket labeled *output (y)* on the other side. Underline *in* and *out* in the words *input* and *output*. Say, *We put something IN to the machine, and we get something OUT.* Say, *If x = 1, how many blocks do I put into the machine?* **one** *What happens inside the machine?* **One more block is added to** *x. How many blocks come out?* **two** *What does y equal?* **two** Change the expression on the function machine and repeat the exercise. Record input and output in function tables.

As you go through each example, teach and model the terms *function, input, output, relation* (the set of ordered pairs as represented in a table). Write the terms on a word wall with examples.

English Language Development Leveled Activities

Entering/Emerging	Developing/Expanding	Bridging
Developing Oral Language	**Number Game**	**Think and Write**
Copy a coordinate plane on one side of a piece of paper. Then copy several function tables on the other side. Laminate enough copies for each student. Distribute. Write the following functions on the board: $4x - 5$, $x + 14$, $x + 7$, $2x - 4$. Tell students to find the output for the following input values (x): 4, 8, 9, 18, 22. Have students use the following sentence frames as they work with a partner on the examples: **The function is _____. The input is _____. The output is _____.** As students' abilities allow, model and prompt the corresponding questions the might ask each other: **What is the function? What is the [input/output]? Is this the [input/output]?**	Write the function $y = 3x - 2$ in a function table on the board. Review the word *function* and ask students which variable is the independent variable (x) or the dependent variable (y). Distribute a number card to each student. Students must look for another student who has a number that makes an input/output match for the function on the board; for example, the numbers 2 and 4 would make a match. Once students have found a match with another student, have them say, **The input is _____. The output is _____.** Then have them write the values in the table. Repeat the process for a different function rule.	Prepare a set of number cards (0–9) and a set of operations cards $(+, -, \cdot, \div)$. Shuffle each pile of cards and place the stacks facedown. Working in pairs, students will choose one number card and one operation card. Using the number, the operation, and the independent variable p, have students write a function and create a function table. Have them describe their functions and function tables, including the input, output, and relations associated with each function.

Teacher Notes:

Lesson 1 Vocabulary
Identify Functions

Use the three-column chart to organize the vocabulary and key words in this lesson. Write the word in Spanish. Then write the definition of each word.

English	Spanish	Definition
function	función	a specific type of relation that assigns exactly <u>one</u> output to each <u>input</u>
input	entrada	the set of <u>x-coordinates</u>
mapping	aplicaciones	A diagram that illustrates how each element of the <u>input</u> is paired with an element in the <u>output</u>.
output	salida	the set of <u>y-coordinates</u>
relation	relación	any set of <u>ordered pairs</u>

Lesson 2 Function Tables

English Learner Instructional Strategy

Language Structure Support: Choral Responses

Write *function, function table, independent variable,* and *dependent variable* and their Spanish cognates, *función, tabla de funciones, variable independiente,* and *variable dependiente,* on the Word Wall with math examples. Have students chorally repeat each word after you model.

When discussing the meaning of *dependent,* underline the base word *depend* and emphasize its relationship to the math meaning of *dependent variable.* Say, *In a function, the value of the output,* **depends** *on the input. The output changes* **depending** *on the input. The value is* **dependent** *on the input.* Then underline the prefix *in-* in *independent.* Tell students the prefix *in-* means "not." Say, *The value of the input, is* **independent**. Stress the *in-* prefix to clearly differentiate it from *dependent.* Say, *It does* **not** *depend on another value.* Ask students to suggest other words they know with the prefix, such as *incorrect, invalid, informal, infrequent.*

English Language Development Leveled Activities

Entering/Emerging	Developing/Expanding	Bridging
Tiered Questions	**Report Back**	**Graffiti Posters**
As students work on problems during the lesson, prompt responses by asking either/or questions or questions that can be answered with a gesture: *Is this the dependent variable or the independent variable?* After the table is filled in, have students identify which column shows the input and which shows the output, either using a gesture or a simple sentence. **This is the [input/ output].**	Have students work in pairs. Randomly assign one problem to each pair. Give pairs time to work together to solve their assigned problems. Display the following sentence frames for students to report back when they have found solutions: **If x is _____, then y is _____. The input is _____. The output is _____.** Then discuss as a group why the output is dependent on the input.	Divide students into four groups and distribute colorful markers and poster paper to each group. Say, *Create a graffiti poster for functions. Use vocabulary you learned in this lesson and provide examples.* Give students time to complete the task. Then have groups post their posters and discuss them. Allow groups to add to their posters as they work through the lesson.

Teacher Notes:

NAME _____ DATE _____ PERIOD _____

Lesson 2 Vocabulary

Function Tables

Use the concept web to describe the different parts of a function table.

Sample answers are given.

Word Bank		
dependent variable	domain	function
	independent variable	range

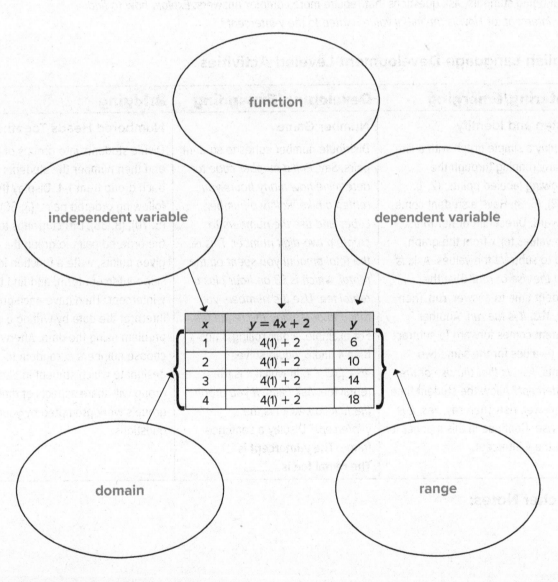

Lesson 3 Construct Linear Functions

English Learner Instructional Strategy

Language Structure Support: Tiered Questions

During the lesson, be sure to ask questions according to ELLs' levels of English proficiency. Ask Entering/Emerging level students simple questions that elicit one-word answers or allow the student to respond with a gesture: *Does this show the value of x or y? Does the point go here or here? Is this the rise or the run? Show me the y-axis.* and so on.

For Developing/Expanding students, ask slightly more complex questions: *Which two points should we choose? If we extend the line across the y-axis, what will we know? When we put the rise over the run, what does that show us?* or *Show me what we do next.*

For Bridging students, ask questions that require more complex answers: *Explain how to find the y-intercept.* or *How is the initial value related to the y-intercept?*

English Language Development Leveled Activities

Entering/Emerging	Developing/Expanding	Bridging
Listen and Identify	**Number Game**	**Numbered Heads Together**
Display a simple graph with a line clearly running through the following labeled points: (2, 1), (4, 2), (6, 3). Have a student come forward. Direct him or her to use two values for *x* from the graph, and to subtract the values. Ask, *Is that the rise or run?* Give the student time to answer. **run** Then say, *Yes, it is the run.* Another student comes forward to subtract the *y*-values for the same two points. Ask, *Is that the rise or the y-intercept?* Allow the student time to answer. **rise** Then say, *Yes, it is the rise.* Continue in this manner to find the *y*-intercept.	Distribute number cubes to student pairs. Say, *Roll a number cube to determine how many hours you rented a bike. Roll two number cubes and use the numbers to create a two-digit number. This is the total amount you spent on the rental, which is $3 an hour plus a rental fee. Use the numbers you rolled to determine the rental fee.* For example, a pair rolling 3 and then 4 and 6 would solve $46 = (3)3 + x$, in which *x* is the rental fee. Ask pairs, *If you graph the function, what is the y-intercept?* Display a sentence frame: **The *y*-intercept is _____. The rental fee is _____.**	Divide students into groups of 4, and then number the students in each group from 1-4. Display the following ordered pairs: (3, 60), (5, 70), (8, 85). Direct groups to use the ordered pairs to graph the given points, write a function in slope-intercept form, and find the *y*-intercept. Then have each group interpret the data by writing a word problem using the data. Afterward, choose numbers at random to designate which student in each group will share aspects of their group's work prompted by your questions.

Teacher Notes:

NAME _____ DATE _____ PERIOD _____

Lesson 3 Notetaking
Construct Linear Functions

Use Cornell notes to better understand the lesson's concepts. Complete each sentence by filling in the blanks with the correct word or phrase.

Questions	Notes
1. What is the initial value of a function?	The initial value of a function is the corresponding _____*y*-value_____ when _____*x*_____ equals _____0_____ .
2. How do I find the initial value of a function?	I find the _____*y*-intercept_____ or I find the value of ____*y*____ when ____$x = 0$____ .

Summary

How is the initial value of a function represented in a table and in a graph? **See students' work.**

_____

_____

_____

_____

_____

_____

_____

Lesson 4 Compare Functions
English Learner Instructional Strategy

Vocabulary Support: Utilize Resources

As students review and utilize previously-taught vocabulary, such as *y-intercept, rate of change, slope, function,* and *equation,* be sure to remind them that they can refer to a glossary or math dictionary for help.

Remind students that many comparisons they will encounter use the *-er* ending, such as *steeper, higher, longer,* and so on, but words with three or more syllables do not. Instead, *more* or *less* are used with these words, as in *more expensive* or *less expensive.*

English Language Development Leveled Activities

Entering/Emerging	Developing/Expanding	Bridging
Frontload Vocabulary	**Sentence Frames**	**Show What You Know**
In addition to the academic vocabulary in this lesson, there is a great deal of non-math vocabulary in examples and exercises. Before students are asked to read or solve a problem, review the vocabulary with them using drawings or photographs. For instance, *high-speed, membership, monthly,* and *remt* can be unfamiliar words to emerging students. Direct students to other translation tools if they are having difficulty with non-math vocabulary or language in the problems.	Assign a problem to student pairs. Give pairs time to solve the problem, and then display the following example sentence frames to help them share their answers: **We know that ____. The variable ___ is the ____, and the variable ___ is ____. The *y*-intercept is ____. The rate of change is ____.** Then say, *Write a function showing the rate of change.* Have pairs complete the task and ask volunteers to share their answers.	Write $y = 8x - 5$ and $y = 6x + 10$. Have students work in pairs. Direct half of the groups to graph the first function, and the other half graph the second function. Then have each group share their graphs with a different group. Have the groups discuss which function has a higher rate of change, and whether it is easier to tell that from the equation or the graph.

Teacher Notes:

NAME _____ DATE _____ PERIOD _____

Lesson 4 Notetaking
Compare Functions

Use the concept web to show representations of the function in different ways.
Use a graph in one of the pieces of the web. Sample answers are given.

Equation

$y = 4x + 2$

Table

x	y
1	6
2	10
3	14
4	18

A store sells tuna salad for $4 a pound. They will deliver any size order for a $2 delivery fee.

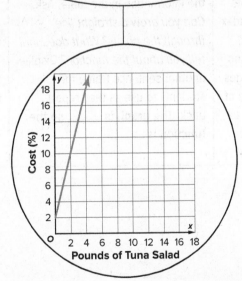

26 Course 3 • Module 5 *Functions*

Lesson 5 Nonlinear Functions
English Learner Instructional Strategy

Graphic Support: Graffiti Poster

Write *nonlinear function* and its Spanish cognate, *función no lineal,* on the Word Wall. Provide a concrete example by displaying a coordinate plane with a nonlinear function graphed on it side-by-side with a coordinate plane showing a linear function.

Begin a graffiti poster. Using colorful markers and large poster paper, creatively write: *linear function.* Invite volunteers to help define the term, list qualities, and draw examples. Then ask students what they hope to learn during the lesson, including what a nonlinear function is and how it is graphed. Have students add this information to the poster. After the lesson, display the following sentence frame and have students use it on the graffiti poster to describe what they learned about nonlinear equations: **I learned that** _____. Encourage students to add to the poster as they gain new knowldge.

English Language Development Leveled Activities

Entering/Emerging	Developing/Expanding	Bridging
Word Knowledge	**Building Oral Language**	**Listen and Write**
Write *linear* and *nonlinear.* Underline the prefix *non-,* and say, *This part of the word means "not."* Nonlinear *means "not linear."* Have students chorally say, **nonlinear.** List word pairs to use in reinforcing the meaning of the prefix: *sense/ nonsense, fiction/nonfiction, violent/nonviolent.* Have students write *linear* on one side of an index card and *nonlinear* on the other. Display tables with data exhibiting constant and nonconstant changes. Ask students to identify the type of function that would correspond to the data by showing the correct term.	Divide students into four small groups and assign a problem to each group. Display the following sentence frame: **The table represents a** _____ **function.** Say, *Use the sentence frame to describe the data.* Then give each group a coordinate plane to use to graph the information in the table. Ask, *Can you draw a straight line through the points? What does that tell you about the function?* Display another sentence frame for students to use as they report back: **The graph is** _____, **so the function is** _____.	Have students work in pairs. Say, *Write a short paragraph describing the relationship between a linear or nonlinear function and how each appears when graphed on a coordinate plane.* Give pairs time to complete the task. Then randomly select one student from each pair to read aloud their paragraph. Work as a group using what students have written to create an anchor chart comparing linear and nonlinear funtions. Post the chart for students to reference.

Teacher Notes:

NAME _____ DATE _____ PERIOD _____

Lesson 5 Vocabulary
Nonlinear Functions

Use the definition map to list qualities about the vocabulary word or phrase.
Sample answers are given.

Vocabulary

nonlinear function

Characteristics

the rate of change is not constant

the graph is not a straight line

can be represented using words, table, graph, in addition to the equation

Description

a function for which the graph is not a straight line

$A = s^2$

$y = x^2 - 1$

$V = s^3$

Write equations of nonlinear functions.

Lesson 6 Qualitative Graphs
English Learner Instructional Strategy

Sensory Support: Photographs

Write *qualitative graph* and its Spanish cognate, *gráfica cualitativa*, on the Word Wall. As you discuss the lesson vocabulary, display photographs of objects or events that you can use to prompt students to think of examples of data that could be recorded in a qualitative graph. For example, a photograph of a sailboat could lead to a graph of the boat's varying speed over time in gusty weather, or a photograph of a hot air balloon could lead to a graph showing its elevation across a distance.

Then have students get into small groups, and give each group a photograph. Have groups create qualitative graphs based on the photographs. Afterward, display the following sentence frames and have students from each group describe their graphs: **The *y*-axis shows _____. The *x*-axis shows _____. The graph shows _____.**

English Language Development Leveled Activities

Entering/Emerging	Developing/Expanding	Bridging
Listen and Identify	**Show What You Know**	**Cooperative Learning**
Display three qualitative graphs labeled A, B, and C, each containing a unique set of graphed data. Give each student three index cards labeled A, B, and C. Then talk about a scenario that could describe one of the graphs. Ask, *Which graph shows this information?* Have students answer by showing the index card with the letter of the graph they choose. Discuss the correct answer.	Display three graphs: one showing a linear function, one showing a quadratic function, and one showing qualitative information. Lead a discussion of how the three graphs are similar to and different from each other. Display sentence frames for students to use during the discussion: **All three graphs _____. The _____ graph and the _____ graph both _____. Only the _____ graph _____.**	Divide students into three groups, and assign a problem to each group. Have the students in each group work together to write a few sentences to answer the Exercise. Then have them refer to the same graph and create another scenario that could be represented by data. Have groups share their new scenarios and justify why the graph represents it.

Teacher Notes:

NAME _____ DATE _____ PERIOD _____

Lesson 6 Vocabulary
Qualitative Graphs

Use the concept web to list characteristics of qualitative graphs. Draw a graph
in one of the pieces of the web. Sample answers are given.

numerical values are
not included

used to represent situations
that may or many not have
numerical values

graph displays the
relationship between the
variables (increasing, no
change, or decreasing)

qualitative graphs

axes are labeled but do not
include numerical values

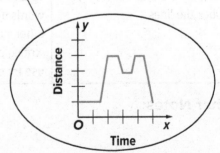

Lesson 1 Solve Systems of Equations by Graphing

English Learner Instructional Strategy

Graphic Support: K-W-L Chart

Write *systems of equations* and its Spanish cognate, *systemas de ecuaciones,* on the Word Wall. Provide a concrete example by displaying a coordinate plane and two linear equations with the same variables. Graph the equations, and then indicate the point of intersection. Remind students that point of intersection is the solution.

Display a K-W-L chart. In the first column, record what students already know about solving systems of equations. In the second column, record what students hope to learn during the lesson, including what parallel lines indicate in a system of equations. After the lesson, display the following sentence frame and have students use it to describe what they learned: **I learned that** _____. Record student responses in the third column of the K-W-L chart.

English Language Development Leveled Activities

Entering/Emerging	Developing/Expanding	Bridging
Word Knowledge	**Signal Words/Phrases**	**Partners Work**
Write *one solution*, *no solution*, and *infinitely many solutions*. Give each student three index cards, and have them copy each phrase on a separate card. Read aloud each phrase, and have students chorally repeat as they hold up the corresponding card, or allow them to simply hold up the card. Show students graphs of lines that either intersect at one point, are parallel, or are the same line. Have students hold up the card that correctly describes the lines.	Review with students how to identify signal words and phrases and then translate them into algebraic equations. Write the following word problems: *1. Sarah has 5 more blocks than Miko has. Sarah has 20 blocks. How many blocks does Miko have? 2. There are twice as many girls as boys. 3. Salim is 10 years older than Lucio. 4. The sum of Gabriela's age and her mother's age is 39.* Have volunteers underline the signal words or phrases, and have the other students guide him or her in writing an algebraic equation to use for solving.	Have students work in pairs on several problems you assign. Give pairs time to solve their assigned problems, then ask them to describe the solution. Display the following sentence frame to help: **There [is/are] _____ solution(s). I know because _____.** Then discuss the relationship between two equations' slopes and the solution. Display these sentence frames to help students: **If the slopes are different, then _____. If the slopes are the same, then _____.**

Teacher Notes:

NAME _____ DATE _____ PERIOD _____

Lesson 1 Vocabulary
Solve Systems of Equations by Graphing

Use the definition map to list qualities about the vocabulary word or phrase.
Sample answers are given.

Vocabulary

system of equations

**Characteristics
of the solution**

Estimate the solution by
graphing on the same
coordinate plane.

Description

a set of two or more
equations with the
same set of variables

solution of the system is
the point of intersection
of the graphs

the solution of the
system satisfies both
equations

$y = mx + b$

$y = nx + c$

$y = 2x + 4$

$y = 7x + 2$

$12 = x + 9y$

$10 = 5x + y$

Examples

Lesson 2 Determine the Number of Solutions

English Learner Instructional Strategy

Collaborative Support: Mentors

Partner each student with another student who is proficient in English. Have the English learner use one of the following sentence frames to ask their proficient partner about the module vocabulary: **What does ____ mean? What is ____?** The partner should define the term in their own words. After the partners work through a problem to determine the number of solutions to a system of equations, have them switch roles and the English-proficient partner asks the question and the English learner defines the term using available language.

English Language Development Leveled Activities

Entering/Emerging	Developing/Expanding	Bridging
Developing Oral Language After the lesson's math concepts have been taught, draw two parallel lines on a coordinate plane. Ask, *Do they have the same slope?* **yes** Ask, *Do they have the same y-intercepts?* **no** Ask, *Is there a solution?* **no** Repeat with another example. As students are able, model and prompt simple sentences: **The [have/do not have] the same slope. They [have/do not have] the same y-intercepts. There (is/are) [no solution/one solution/infinite solutions].**	**Building Oral Language** Review and practice question formation. Write the following frames on the board: **Do the ____ have the same ____? The y-intercepts are ____ . Is there a ____? How many ____ are there?** For each problem that partners are working on, have one partner ask a simple question and the partner give a simple sentence in response.	**Exploring Language Structures** Remind students that they need to know the slope of the line and the y-intercept to determine what solutions are possible. Once those are identified, have them practice using If/Then statements to describe how they can determine the number of solutions for a system of equations. Write the frame, **If two equations have the [same slope/different slope] and [the same/different] y-intercepts, then ____.** Sample response: **If two equations have the same slope and the same y-intercepts, then there are infinite solutions to the system of equations.**

Teacher Notes:

NAME _____ DATE _____ PERIOD _____

Lesson 2 Vocabulary
Determine Number of Solutions

Use the three-column chart to organize the vocabulary and key words in this lesson.
Write the word in Spanish. Then write the definition of each word.

English	Spanish	Definition
equation	ecuación	A mathematical sentence stating that two quantities are ___equal___
slope	pendiente	The rate of change between any _two points_ on a line. The ratio of the vertical change (_rise_) over the horizontal change (_run_).
slope-intercept form	forma pendiente intersección	An equation written in the form $y = mx + b$, where m is the _slope_ and b is the _y-intercept_
solution	solución	Any value that satisfies an _equation_
y-intercept	intersección y	The y-coordinate of the point where the _line_ crosses the _y_-axis

Lesson 3 Solve Systems of Equations by Substitution

English Learner Instructional Strategy

Vocabulary Support: Sentence Frames

Write *substitution* and its Spanish cognate, *sustitución*, on the Word Wall. Describe non-math examples of *substitution*, such as in a recipe or when a substitute teaches the class. Relate these examples to the math meaning.

Display the following sentence frames to help students participate during the lesson:

Entering/Emerging: **y equals _____. x equals _____. The solution is _____.**

Developing/Expanding: **I can substitute _____ with _____. I can rewrite _____ as _____. The solution of the system is _____.**

Bridging: **I know _____, therefore _____. The solution of the system is _____, so _____.**

English Language Development Leveled Activities

Entering/Emerging	Developing/Expanding	Bridging
Exploring Language Structures Display the following sentence frames: **I will substitute _____ for _____. I am substituting _____ for _____. I substituted _____ for _____.** As you model solving a practice exercise, use the sentence frames to narrate what you are doing. Point to the appropriate sentence and use it as you describe the substitution you will make, then as you are actually doing it, and finally to describe what you just did. Have volunteers use the sentence frames as they guide you through more examples.	**Listen and Write** Have students work in pairs. Assign a problem for pairs to solve. Say, *Tell your partner each step he or she must follow to solve the system of equations.* As one student in each pair describes how to solve, the other student will follow the directions and solve the system of equations on an index card. Ask volunteers to share their answers. Then assign a new problem and have students switch roles.	**Word Knowledge** Write a list of sequence words: *first, second, then, next, last, finally,* and so on. Have students work in small groups. Say, *Write a short paragraph describing how to use substitution to solve a system of equations.* Give students time to complete the task. Choose a student from each group to read aloud his or her group's paragraph. Then lead a discussion comparing and contrasting groups' paragraphs and determining which one is the easiest to understand and/or is the best written.

Teacher Notes:

NAME _____ DATE _____ PERIOD _____

Lesson 3 Vocabulary
Solve Systems of Equations by Substitution

Use the word cards to define each vocabulary word or phrase and give an example. Sample answers are given.

Word Cards

substitution

Definition

an algebraic model that can be
used to find the exact solutions
of a system of equations

Example Sentence

Use substitution to replace y with $3x$ in the second equation
to solve the system of equations $y = 3x$ and $y = 4x + 2$.

sustitución

Definición

modelo algebraico que se puede
usar para calcular la solución
exacta de un systema de ecuaciones

Word Cards

variable

Definition

a symbol used to represent a
number in expressions or
sentences

Example Sentence

The variables x and y are used in the system of equations
$y = 3x$ and $y = 4x + 2$.

variable

Definición

un símboloque se usa para
representar númerous en
expresiones o enunciados

Course 3 · Module 6 *Systems of Linear Equations* **31**

Lesson 4 Solve Systems of Equations by Elimination

English Learner Instructional Strategy

Language Structure Support: Multiple-Meaning Words

Write *eliminate* and *elimination* and their cognates *eliminar* and *la eliminación* on the board. Have students discuss what they think these words mean. Allow them to share any ideas. Write them on the board. Tell students that, in addition to its math meaning *eliminate* can have several, though closely related, meanings. It can mean "to get rid of" or "to defeat." Offer examples of alternative usage, such as *Casey wanted to eliminate sugar from his diet. The Blue Jays eliminated the Red Sox from the tournament.*

English Language Development Leveled Activities

Entering/Emerging	Developing/Expanding	Bridging
Look and Identify	**Partners Work/Pairs Share**	**Show What You Know**
Write the following system of equations: $2x + 5y = 14$ and $3x - 5y = 11$. Point to $5y$ and $-5y$. Say, *I want to eliminate the variable y. Do I add or subtract?* **add** Perform the next step to eliminate y. Ask, *Did I eliminate y?* **yes** Then solve for x. Now that you have x, substitute x into one of the equations and solve for y. Repeat for other systems.	Assign a system of functions to each pair and have them solve the system of equations, discussing the reasoning for their steps as they go. Once they have solved the system, have each pair turn and review their work with another pair and compare any differences in how the pairs solved their system, if any. Suggest these communication guides: **Oh, you ____ instead of ____? We didn't think of that. It looks like we forgot to ____. It looks like we ____, just like you did.** Monitor students as they work, and share with the whole group a few of the interesting pieces of discussion you heard.	When it is time to review work as a group, have a Bridging student lead the review. Have them ask questions of their peers, elicit certain answers by giving clues or asking leading questions, and then demonstrate the proper procedure for solving the problem as needed. Make sure they also confirm that their "students" understand by asking, **What questions do you have?**

Teacher Notes:

NAME _____ DATE _____ PERIOD _____

Lesson 4 Notetaking
Solve Systems of Equations by Elimination

Use Cornell notes to better understand the lesson's concepts. Complete each sentence by filling in the blanks with the correct word or phrase.

Questions	Notes
1. What is the elimination method for solving a system of equations?	Elimination is when I use addition or subtraction to eliminate one ___variable___ in a ___system of equations___. In a system of equations, if both equations have a like variable with the same ___coefficient___, then elimination can be used to solve for the other ___variable___.
2. How can I solve systems of equations using elimination?	First, I align ___like___ terms. Next, I add or subtract to ___eliminate___ one variable. Then I solve for the other variable. Finally, I ___substitute___ the value of the variable I found in one of the ___equations___ to find the value of the other variable.

Summary

Do you prefer using substitution or elimination to solve a system of equations? Explain. **See students' work.**

_____

_____

_____

_____

_____

_____

_____

Lesson 5 Write and Solve Systems of Equations

English Learner Instructional Strategy

Vocabulary Support: Making Connections

Write each of the following vocabulary terms at the top of separate sheets of paper: *rise, run, slope, slope-intercept form, substitution, elimination, solution, systems of equations, x-intercept, y-intercept.* Lay the papers out on a table or tape them up, and then briefly review their meanings. As students work through the examples and problems, challenge them to look for opportunities to use each term or to identify examples of each term. When you hear a student use a vocabulary word or the student identifies an example, direct the student to write his or her name on the corresponding sheet of paper. Reward the first student who uses all ten terms, perhaps by allowing him or her to skip any clean-up activities.

English Language Development Leveled Activities

Entering/Emerging	Developing/Expanding	Bridging
Developing Oral Language	**Report Back**	**Communication Guides**
Divide students into two groups. Write a system of equations, such as $y = x + 3$ and $y = 2x$. Direct one group to solve using a coordinate plane and the other group to solve algebraically. Ask each group to share their solution. **(3, 6)** Ask, *Were the solutions the same or different?* **same** Write another system of equations, and have groups switch solving methods. Remind students to name module vocabulary as they encounter it.	Write a system of equations, such as $2x + y = 22$ and $x - y = 14$. Have partners solve the system algebraically. Ask each pair to share their solution. **(12, −2)** Then ask, *How can you check that your answer is correct?* Have two pairs consult with each other and work out the language to respond. Ask a volunteer from each group to report back to the whole group. **I can substitute the x and y values into the equations to see it the values make both equations true.**	Students have learned how to solve systems of equations in multiple ways. When they are working on review or test preparation, have students work together to solve problems and have them tell which method, including substitution or elimination, they would use and why. Suggest frames such as **I see there are ____, so I would use ____ to solve this system of equations. I would use ____ for this problem because ____.**

Teacher Notes:

NAME _____ DATE _____ PERIOD _____

Lesson 5 Review Vocabulary
Write and Solve Systems of Equations

Use the flow chart to review the process for writing a system of equations.
Sample answers are given.

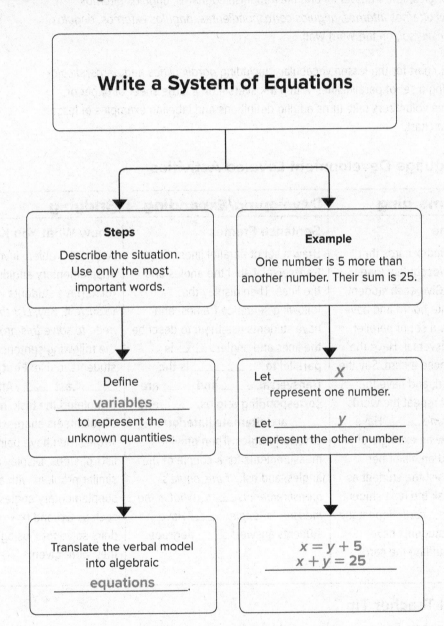

Write a System of Equations

Steps

Describe the situation.
Use only the most
important words.

Example

One number is 5 more than
another number. Their sum is 25.

Define
variables
to represent the
unknown quantities.

Let _____ x _____
represent one number.

Let _____ y _____
represent the other number.

Translate the verbal model
into algebraic
equations .

$x = y + 5$
$x + y = 25$

Course 3 • Module 6 *Systems of Linear Equations* **33**

Lesson 1 Angle Relationships and Parallel Lines

English Learner Instructional Strategy

Graphic Support: Anchor Chart

Write *alternate exterior angles*, *alternate interior angles*, *corresponding angles*, *exterior angles*, *interior angles*, and *transversal* and their Spanish cognates, *ángulos alternos externos*, *ángulos alternos internos*, *ángulos correspondientes*, *ángulos externos*, *ángulos internos*, and *transversal*, on the Word Wall.

Create an anchor chart for the lesson vocabulary, including *parallel lines* and *perpendicular lines*. After drawing a set of parallel lines with a transversal on a large sheet of paper or poster board, have volunteers take turns adding definitions and labeling examples of lesson vocabulary on the chart.

English Language Development Leveled Activities

Entering/Emerging	Developing/Expanding	Bridging
Number Game	**Sentence Frames**	**Show What You Know**
Create a set of index cards that contain lesson vocabulary (one term per card). Give each student an erasable white board and have them each draw a set of parallel lines with a transversal. Have the first student choose a card. Say the word on the card, and have the student chorally repeat the word. Then say, *Show me _____.* Have the student draw an example of the vocabulary word on his or her white board. Assist the student as needed. Then ask the next student in line to choose a card. Repeat the activity until all students have had a turn, reshuffling the cards as needed.	Draw a set of parallel lines with a transversal. Label the angles and the lines. Then display the following sentence frames, and have students use them to describe the lines and angles: _____ **is parallel to** _____. _____ **is the transversal.** _____ **and** _____ **are corresponding angles.** _____ **and** _____ **are alternate [interior/ exterior] angles.** Then provide measurements for a couple of the angles, and ask, *If this angle's measurement is _____, what is the measure of angle _____?* Have students answer: _____ **degrees.**	Assign a problem involving using supplementary angles to solve for *x*. Have students work in pairs to solve it. Say, *List the steps you need to solve this problem.* Display the following sentence frames for students to use: **First** _____. **Then** _____. **Last** _____. After pairs have completed the task, have a couple of volunteers share what they wrote. Then have pairs exchange lists of steps. Display another similar problem with a pair of supplementary angles labeled, such as $6x°$ and $(x + 5)°$. Have pairs solve for *x* using the steps they were given.

Multicultural Teacher Tip

Encourage ELLs to share traditions, stories, songs, or other aspects of their native culture with the other students in class. You might even create a "culture wall" where all students can display cultural items. This will help create a classroom atmosphere of respect and appreciation for all cultures, and in turn, will create a more comfortable learning environment for ELLs.

Lesson 1 Vocabulary

Angle Relationships and Parallel Lines

Use the three-column chart to write the vocabulary word and definition for each drawing. Sample answers are given.

What I See	Vocabulary Word	Definition
	perpendicular lines	two lines that intersect to form right angles
	parallel lines	Lines in the same plane that never intersect or cross; the symbol ∥ means parallel.
	transversal	a line that intersects two or more other lines
	interior angles	the four inside angles formed when two lines are cut by a transversal
	exterior angles	the four outer angles formed when two lines are cut by a transversal
	alternate interior angles	interior angles that lie on opposite sides of the transversal
	alternate exterior angles	exterior angles that lie on opposite sides of the transversal
	corresponding angles	angles that are in the same position on two lines in relation to a transversal

Lesson 2 Angle Relationships and Triangles
English Learner Instructional Strategy

Sensory Support: Manipulatives

Write *triangle* and its Spanish cognate, *triángulo,* on the Word Wall, along with examples of different kinds of triangles to provide concrete examples. As students refer to *triangles* and *angles* during the lesson, listen for the final /z/ sound indicating plural. If the final *s* is being said as /s/, model the correct pronunciation and have students repeat.

Divide students into four groups. Distribute a different triangle to each group, along with a protractor. Have students trace their triangles onto paper. Say, *Use the protractor to measure two angles of your triangle. Write each measurement by the angle. For the third angle, write* x. Have groups exchange papers. Then say, *Find the value of* x *in the triangle you were given.* Display sentence frames for students to use in sharing their answers: **The given angles' measures are _____. The value of *x* is _____.** Be sure students are differentiating between *are* and *is* correctly to demonstrate understanding of singular and plural verbs.

English Language Development Leveled Activities

Entering/Emerging	Developing/Expanding	Bridging
Word Knowledge	**Academic Word Knowledge**	**Communication Guide**
Write *remote* in a word web. Fill in the rest of the web with synonyms for *remote,* such as *far, distant, not close, not nearby.* Display a triangle with a side extended and the exterior angle and interior angles labeled *a, b, c,* and *d.* Indicate the exterior angle, and then point to the remote angles as you say, *These angles are farther away. They are the remote angles.* Then create a two-column chart labeled *Interior* and *Exterior.* Fill the chart with student examples of objects found inside and outside a building or home.	Create several three-card sets with the following math vocabulary: *interior angle, exterior angle, remote interior angles.* Randomly distribute one card to each student. Have students get into groups of three based on the card sets, and give each group a protractor. Say, *Draw a triangle. Extend one side. Use the protractor to measure the angles.* Then ask each student to say the measurement of the angle or angles referred to on the card. Display the following sentence frames: **The measure of _____ angle is _____ degrees. The measure of _____ angles are _____ and _____.**	Have students work in small groups to create guides for classifying triangles. Each page should feature one type of triangle, including its name, a sentence describing it, and a visual example and non-example. List the following types of triangles: *obtuse, acute, right, equilateral, isosceles,* and *scalene.* Provide the following sentence frames for students to use: **A _____ triangle has _____. The sum of the angle measures in this triangle is _____.** Add the guides to a student reference library so they are available for future use.

Teacher Notes:

NAME _____ DATE _____ PERIOD _____

Lesson 2 Vocabulary
Angle Relationships and Triangles

Use the vocabulary squares to write a definition and a sentence. Then label the
figure with an example for each vocabulary word. Sample answers are given.

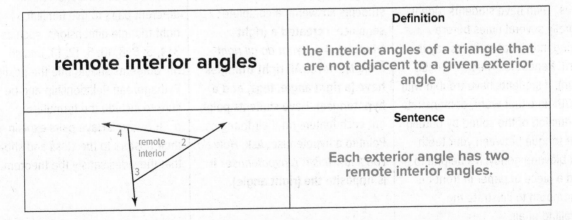

	Definition
interior angle	the angle formed by the segments that lie inside the triangle
	Sentence
	A triangle has three interior angles.

	Definition
exterior angle	the angle formed by one side of the triangle and the extension of the adjacent side
	Sentence
	A triangle has three exterior angle.

	Definition
remote interior angles	the interior angles of a triangle that are not adjacent to a given exterior angle
	Sentence
	Each exterior angle has two remote interior angles.

Lesson 3 The Pythagorean Theorem
English Learner Instructional Strategy

Sensory Support: Real-World Examples

Write *hypotenuse* and *Pythagorean Theorem* and their Spanish cognates, *hipotenusa* and *Teorema de Pitágoras*, on the Word Wall. Briefly introduce the meaning of each word, and then during the lesson, frequently refer to the Word Wall to reinforce meaning and provide concrete examples for each word. Have students wander the classroom and collect at least one good example of a right triangle. Have students identify the right angle, the legs, and the hypotenuse. (The hypotenuse may be imaginary; for example, if students use the corner of a desk as their right angle, then they may use a straightedge or a piece of string to create the hypotenuse.) Have students present their examples to the group and point out each feature to classmates.

Say, *Measure each side of the triangle. Use the measurements in the Pythagorean theorem to show that the triangle is a right triangle.* Have students round to the nearest centimeter. Give pairs time to complete the task. Then display the following sentence frames to help them share what they found: **The legs are ____ centimeters and ____ centimeters. The hypotenuse is ____ centimeters. ____ squared plus ____ squared equals ____ squared. It is a right triangle.**

English Language Development Leveled Activities

Entering/Emerging	Developing/Expanding	Bridging
Phonemic Awareness	**Building Oral Language**	**Anchor Charts**
English learners may have trouble with pronunciation of the lesson vocabulary. Model *hypotenuse* (high PAH tih noos). Have students repeat chorally and then individually. Model *Pythagorean* (puh THAG uh REE uhn) several times. Then have students repeat chorally several times before having individual students say the word. Repeat for *Theorem* (THEE ruhm). If students have trouble with the /th/ in either word, demonstrate production of the sound by putting your tongue between your teeth and blowing gently. It's helpful to hold a piece of paper in front on your mouth to illustrate the expelling of air.	On a regular piece of paper, have students draw any straight line from one side edge of the paper to the top or bottom edge. Then have them color the line and both edges of the paper. Ask, *What type of triangle did you create?* Have students answer in a complete sentence: **I created a (right triangle).** Ask, *What do all right triangles have?* **All right triangles have (a right angle, legs, and a hypotenuse).** Have students point out each feature on their triangles. Point to a hypotenuse. Ask, *How do you know this is a hypotenuse?* **It is opposite the (right angle).**	Have student pairs make anchor charts about right triangles and the Pythagorean relationship. Posters should include a diagram of a right triangle with the terms leg and hypotenuse labeling the sides, as well as the dimensions. Assign different pairs to use familiar right triangle dimensions, such as 3, 4, 5; 6, 8, 10; 5, 12, 13; and so on. Students should title the poster Pythagorean Relationship and be sure to include the formula: $a^2 + b^2 = c^2$. Have pairs explain their posters to the class and show that the sides satisfy the theorem.

NAME _____ DATE _____ PERIOD _____

Lesson 3 Vocabulary
The Pythagorean Theorem

Use the vocabulary squares to write a definition, a sentence, and an example for each vocabulary word.   Sample answers are given.

legs	**Definition** the sides of a right triangle that form the right angle
Example 	**Sentence** There are two legs in a right triangle.

hypotenuse	**Definition** the side opposite the right angle in a right triangle
Example 	**Sentence** The hypotenuse in a right triangle is the longest side.

Pythagorean Theorem	**Definition** In a right triangle, the square of the length of the hypotenuse *c* is equal to the sum of the squares of the lengths of the legs *a* and *b*.
Example If a triangle is a right triangle, then $a^2 + b^2 = c^2$	**Sentence** When you know two lengths of the three sides of a right triangle, you can use the Pythagorean Theorem to find the unknown side length.

Lesson 4 Converse of the Pythagorean Theorem

English Learner Instructional Strategy

Language Structure Support: Modeled Talk

Write *converse* and ask students if they know a non-math meaning for the term. Say, *If I converse* [emphasize the stress on the second syllable] *with someone, I talk with them.* **Converse** *is a verb.* Then say, *The math meaning of* **converse** [emphasize the stress on the first syllable] *is different. A* **converse** *is when you switch the parts of a conditional statement. In math,* **converse** *is a noun.* Write: *If it is a turtle, it has four legs, a tail, and a hard, round shell.* Then write, *If it has four legs, a tail, and a hard, round shell, it is a turtle.* Point to the second sentence and say, *the converse.* Have students chorally repeat **converse.** Be sure they are stressing the first syllable.

English Language Development Leveled Activities

Entering/Emerging	Developing/Expanding	Bridging
Look and Identify	**Exploring Language Structure**	**Logical Reasoning**
Draw a right triangle. Label the sides *leg, leg,* and *hypotenuse.* Point to *leg* and *hypotenuse.* Ask, *Which word is longer?* Have students answer. Then ask, *Which side is longest?* Have students answer. Say, *The longest word is the longest side.* Draw a stick figure. Label each leg. Point to the figure and the triangle and say, *The triangle and the man stand on legs.* Then draw the stick figure upside down and a right triangle with the hypotenuse at the bottom. Label the legs in both. Say, *Even in a different position, these are still the legs.*	Review language for comparison using right triangles. Display a right triangle and have students tell what they know about it, including labeling its parts. Say, *Compare the hypotenuse to the leg.* Model and prompt the frame **The ____ is [longer/shorter] than the ____. ____ is the [longest/shortest] side of the triangle.** Compare the size of the angles in the same way using *larger* and *smaller.* Then teach the question form of the frames: **Which side is ____? Which angle is ____?** Have partners ask and answer questions.	Review the Pythagorean Theorem: If a triangle is a right triangle, then $a^2 + b^2 = c^2$. The converse of the Pythagorean Theorem is also true: If sides $a^2 + b^2 = c^2$, then the triangle is a right triangle. Ask students to say other if/then statements and identify which ones are true and which are not. Share this example: *If it is 7 a.m., then it is morning.* The converse of the sentence is: *If it is morning, then it is 7 a.m.* Ask, *Is the converse true?* **no** Have students think of other examples, and challenge them to find examples for which the statement and its converse are both true.

Teacher Notes:

NAME _____ DATE _____ PERIOD _____

Lesson 4 Vocabulary

Converse of the Pythagorean Theorem

Use the definition map to list qualities about the vocabulary word or phrase.
Sample answers are given.

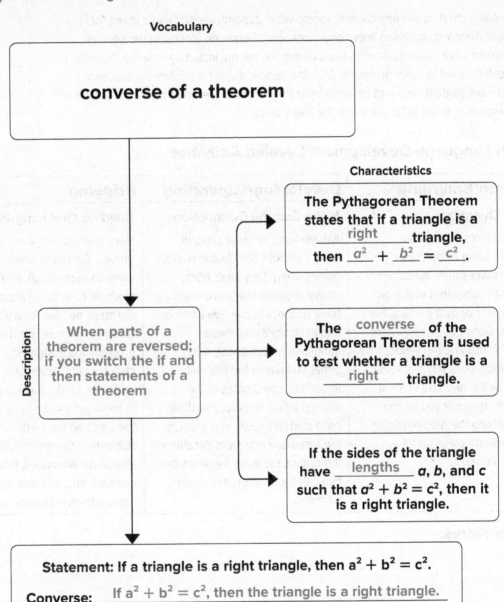

Vocabulary

converse of a theorem

Description

When parts of a theorem are reversed; if you switch the if and then statements of a theorem

Characteristics

The Pythagorean Theorem states that if a triangle is a ___right___ triangle, then $a^2 + b^2 = c^2$.

The ___converse___ of the Pythagorean Theorem is used to test whether a triangle is a ___right___ triangle.

If the sides of the triangle have ___lengths___ a, b, and c such that $a^2 + b^2 = c^2$, then it is a right triangle.

Statement: If a triangle is a right triangle, then $a^2 + b^2 = c^2$.

Converse: ___If $a^2 + b^2 = c^2$, then the triangle is a right triangle.___

Write the converse of the Pythagorean Theorem.

Course 3 · Module 7 *Triangles and the Pythagorean Theorem* **37**

Lesson 5 Distance on the Coordinate Plane
English Learner Instructional Strategy

Graphic Support: K-W-L Chart

Write *Distance Formula* and its Spanish cognate, *fórmula de la distancia,* on the Word Wall. Provide a concrete example by displaying a coordinate plane and a linear equation, and then using the formula to find the distance between two coordinates along the line.

Display a K-W-L chart. In the first column, record what students already know about the Pythagorean Theorem, graphing linear equations, and coordinate planes. In the second column, record what students hope to learn during the lesson, including how the Distance Formula can be used to solve problems. After the lesson, display the following sentence frame and have students use it to describe what they learned: **I learned that _____.** Record student responses in the third column of the K-W-L chart.

English Language Development Leveled Activities

Entering/Emerging	Developing/Expanding	Bridging
Tiered Questions Guide students through the examples using a coordinate plane and by asking simple questions that can be answered with a one-word answer or by a gesture. For example, *Does this point go here or here? Is this line the hypotenuse c, or is it this line? Will this show the rise or the run?* Use student responses to guide you as you model solving the problem using the coordinate plane and the Distance Formula.	**Make Cultural Connections** Ask students to name cities in other countries they know, perhaps places where they were born, where relatives live, or where they have visited. Choose two cities and find each city's coordinates (longitude and latitude), using either an atlas or the Internet. Round the coordinates to the nearest whole degree, and then have students guide you in using the Distance Formula to determine the distance in miles between the two cities (one degree is about 53 miles).	**Building Oral Language** Have students work in small groups. Distribute several index cards to each group, and direct students to write an explanation of the steps needed for using the Distance Formula to solve a problem you assign. Say, *Write one step per card.* Then have groups exchange cards. Have the students in each group take turns reading the steps on the cards while other students in the group follow the directions. Afterward, have groups compare answers and critique the explanations they were given.

Teacher Notes:

NAME _____ DATE _____ PERIOD _____

Lesson 5 Notetaking

Distance on the Coordinate Plane

Use the flow chart to review the processes for finding the distance between two points on a coordinate plane. Sample answers are given.

> ## Use the Pythagorean Theorem or Distance Formula to find the distance between two points on a coordinate plane.
>
>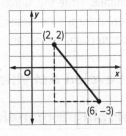

State the Pythagorean Theorem.	State the Distance Formula.
$a^2 + b^2 = c^2$	$d = \sqrt{(x_2 - x_1)^2 + (y_2 - x_1)^2}$

Find the length of the segment using the Pythagorean Theorem.	Find the length of the segment using the Distance Formula.
$a^2 + b^2 = c^2$	$c = \sqrt{(6-2)^2 + (-3-2)^2}$
$4^2 + 5^2 = c^2$	$= \sqrt{4^2 + (-5)^2}$
$16 + 25 = c^2$	$= \sqrt{16 + 25}$
$\sqrt{41} = c$ or about 6.4 units	$= \sqrt{41}$
	≈ 6.4

38   **Course 3 · Module 7** *Triangles and the Pythagorean Theorem*

Lesson 1 Translations

English Learner Instructional Strategy

Language Structure Support: Affixes

Write *transformation, translation, image,* and *congruent* and their Spanish cognates, *transformación, traslación, imagen,* and *congruente,* on the Word Wall. Briefly introduce the meaning of each word, and then, during the lesson, frequently refer to the Word Wall to reinforce meaning and provide concrete examples for each term.

Write *preimage,* underline the prefix *pre-,* and say, *This word part means "before." The preimage is the image **before** it is transformed.* Write *pre-* in a word web, and have students suggest other words they know with the prefix, such as *preview, preteen, prepay, preheat.* Then create a two-column chart labeled *Verb* and *Noun.* Write *transform, transformation, translate,* and *translation* in their respective columns. Write the suffix *-tion* and say, *This word part changes a verb to a noun.* Have students brainstorm other examples to add to the chart, such as *act/action, collect/collection, connect/connection,* and so on.

English Language Development Leveled Activities

Entering/Emerging	Developing/Expanding	Bridging
Academic Vocabulary	**Anchor Charts**	**Partners Work**
Have students get into small groups and use a glossary and translation tools to review the lesson's math vocabulary. Direct students to write definitions for the terms in their math notebooks and provide visual examples. Allow students to write the definitions in their own words and/or in their native languages. For *transformation,* be sure students include examples of *slide, flip,* and *turn.* Afterward, regroup students and have them share what they wrote in their journals with the students in another group.	Divide students into four groups. Say, *Make an anchor chart showing different kinds of transformations.* Each chart should include a title at the top of the poster and several labeled examples of different transformations. When the charts are completed, have groups display and describe their charts. Each group's description should use each lesson vocabulary word at least once. List the words for students' reference: *transformation, translation, congruent, image, preimage.*	Have students work in pairs. Have each pair draw a triangle on a coordinate plane, making sure each point lands where two lines intersect. Then have pairs trade papers. Say, *Translate the figure on the plane. Be sure the new image is congruent to the preimage.* Afterward, have students describe the change in coordinates after the translation. Display the following sentence frames: **The coordinates of the preimage were _____. After we translated the figure, the coordinates became _____.**

Teacher Notes:

NAME _____ DATE _____ PERIOD _____

Lesson 1 Vocabulary
Translations

Use the three-column chart to organize the vocabulary in this lesson. Write the
word in Spanish. Then write the definition of each word. Sample answers are given.

English	Spanish	Definition
transformation	transformación	an operation that maps a geometric figure, the preimage, onto a new figure, the image
preimage	preimagen	the original figure before a transformation
image	imagen	the resulting figure after a transformation
translation	traslación	a transformation that slides a figure from one position to another without turning
congruent	congruente	if one image can be obtained by another by a sequence of rotation, reflection, or translations

Lesson 2 Reflections

English Learner Instructional Strategy

Language Structure Support: Modeled Talk

Write *reflection* and *line of reflection* and their Spanish cognates, *reflexión* and *linea de reflexión,* on the Word Wall. Display a mirror and use it to discuss the non-math meaning of *reflection.* Then place the mirror along one of the axes of a coordinate plane. Draw a figure on the plane, and point out how the figure appears to be "reflected" to the opposite side of the axis.

During the lesson, be sure to model clear and correct English pronunciation for students. Whenever possible, have students chorally repeat key words and phrases after you have modeled saying them. Display the following sentence frames to help students during the lesson: **The coordinates are _____. _____ is the line of reflection. The reflection is over the _____.** Be sure students are using subject-verb agreement in differentiating between *is* and *are.* Correct usage as necessary by modeling and then having the student echo.

English Language Development Leveled Activities

Entering/Emerging	Developing/Expanding	Bridging
Choral Responses	**Building Oral Language**	**Academic Word Knowledge**
Give each student an index card. Direct students to write *x-axis* on one side of the card and *y-axis* on the other. As you model reflecting figures across different axes, ask, *Which axis is the line of reflection?* Have students answer by showing you the corresponding side of the index card. Say the answer aloud, *The _____ is the line of reflection,* and have students chorally repeat. After completing multiple examples, draw a figure on the coordinate plane and have a volunteer come forward to complete a reflection per your instruction.	Divide students into groups of four and give each group a blank coordinate plane. Then have the students take turns performing the following tasks: 1) *Draw a three- or four-sided figure within a single quadrant.* 2) *Write the coordinates of the figure.* 3) *Choose an axis as the line of reflection.* 4) *Determine the reflected image's coordinates.* 5) *Use the new coordinates to draw the reflected image and determine correctness.* After groups have completed the tasks, have each student use math vocabulary to describe the step they completed.	Have students work in pairs to write rules for how coordinates change depending over which axis a figure is reflected. Display the following sentence frame for students to use: **When a figure is reflected over the _____, the _____ coordinate stays the same.** Have students share the rules they wrote, and then say, *Write the rules in your math notebook so you can refer to them in the future.*

Teacher Notes:

NAME _____ DATE _____ PERIOD _____

Lesson 2 Vocabulary
Reflections

Use the word cards to define each vocabulary word or phrase and give an example. Sample answers are given.

Word Cards

reflection

Definition

a transformation where a

figure is flipped over a line

_____

Example Sentence

A reflection creates a mirror image of the original figure.

When you look in the mirror, you see your reflection.

reflexión

Definición

transformación en la cual una

figura se voltea sobre una

recta

línea de reflexión

Word Cards

line of reflection

Definition

the line over which a figure is

reflected

_____

_____

Example Sentence

In a reflection, each point of the preimage and its image, are

the same distance from the line of reflection.

línea de reflexión

Definición

línea a través de la cual se

refleja una figura

Lesson 3 Rotations

English Learner Instructional Strategy

Collaborative Support: Numbered Heads Together

Write *rotation* and *rotational symmetry* and their Spanish cognates, *rotación* and *simetría rotacional*, on the Word Wall. Provide meanings and concrete examples for the vocabulary.

Organize students into groups of four and number students as 1–4. Assign one problem to each group. They should discuss the problem, agree on a solution, and ensure that everyone in the group understands and can give the answer. Afterward, call out a random number from 1 to 4. Have students assigned to that number raise their hands, and when called on, answer for their team.

Display the following sentence frames for students who need additional help:
I don't understand _____. What does _____ mean? I need help with _____.

English Language Development Leveled Activities

Entering/Emerging	Developing/Expanding	Bridging
Number Game	**Report Back**	**Pass the Pen**
Write: *1) clockwise* and *2) counterclockwise*. Divide students into two teams. Place an object with rotational symmetry onto a table, and have a student from one of the teams come forward. Have the students of the other team choose a direction (clockwise or counterclockwise) and chorally say either **1** or **2**, or say **clockwise/ counterclockwise.** The student scores a point for his or her team by turning the object in the correct direction. Have teams take turns giving directions and following directions. Continue until one team has 5 points.	Create a set of cards describing rotations, such as *90° clockwise about a point; 180° counterclockwise about the origin;* and so on. Have students pair up, and then randomly distribute one card to each pair. Direct students to draw a figure on a coordinate plane and then rotate the figure according to what is shown on the card they received. Have pairs exchange graphs (but not cards) and then describe the rotation on the coordinate plane they were given using the following sentence frame: **The figure has been rotated _____ degrees about [a/the] _____.**	Divide students into four groups and assign a problem to each group. Have students work jointly on the problem by passing a copy of the problem around the table to complete each step. Direct each member of the group to write a sentence or phrase on a strip of paper describing the step he or she has completed. Afterward, have groups share their work, and have each student read the sentence they wrote.

Teacher Notes:

NAME _____ DATE _____ PERIOD _____

Lesson 3 Vocabulary
Rotations

Use the concept web to name the transformation and the parts of the transformation. Sample answers are given.

Word Bank	
center of rotation	image
preimage	rotation

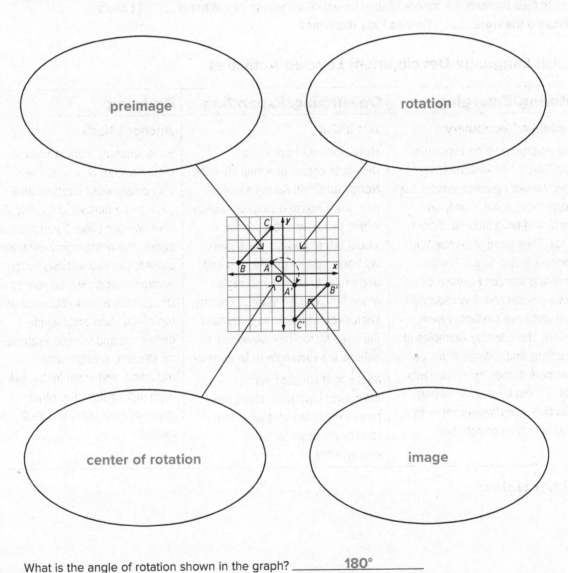

(preimage)

(rotation)

(center of rotation)

(image)

What is the angle of rotation shown in the graph? _____ 180° _____

Course 3 · Module 8 *Transformations* **41**

Lesson 4 Dilations

English Learner Instructional Strategy

Vocabulary Support: Build Background Knowledge

To support students' vocabulary acquisition on a regular basis, encourage them to scan their texts to identify words that are unfamiliar. Have students read the words aloud or, if they are unsure of pronunciation, by spelling the words. Create a list of the words, and then review each by having students refer to a glossary, their math notebook, the Word Wall, the classroom anchor charts, or other reference sources.

If Entering/Emerging students have difficulty with non-math vocabulary during the lesson, encourage them to ask more proficient English-speaking peers for help. Display sentence frames to help students ask for clarification for unfamiliar vocabulary: **What is _____? I don't understand the word _____. How do I say this word?**

English Language Development Leveled Activities

Entering/Emerging	Developing/Expanding	Bridging
Academic Vocabulary	**Act It Out**	**Anchor Charts**
Write *enlargement* and underline *large*. Say, *If I make something larger, I make an enlargement.* Say *enlargement* again, slowly and clearly, and have student chorally repeat. Then write *reduction* and underline *reduc*. Say, *If I make something smaller, I reduce its size. I make a reduction.* Say *reduction* again and have students repeat chorally. Then display examples of reductions and enlargements on coordinate planes. Have students identify them by chorally saying **reduction** or **enlargement** or by pointing to the correct word.	Have students work in pairs. Distribute copies of a map showing North and South America to each pair. Say, *Choose a state or country where you have lived, visited, or would like to go visit.* Have pairs lay tracing paper on the map and use a ruler to draw a rectangle around the chosen state or country. Then direct students to determine the scale factor they would use to enlarge the rectangle to fill most of an $8\frac{1}{2} \times 11$ sheet of paper. Afterward, have pairs share the place they chose and why, and identify the scale factor of enlargement.	Have students work in pairs to create anchor charts for the vocabulary word *dilation*. Give each pair a number cube. Say, *Roll your number cube. If you roll 1, roll again. The number you roll is the scale factor you will use for the enlargement shown on your chart.* Direct pairs to write *Dilations* at the top of the chart and include definitions and labeled examples for *dilation, enlargement, reduction,* and *scale factor*. Ask each pair to show the other students their chart and justify their examples.

Teacher Notes:

NAME _____ DATE _____ PERIOD _____

Lesson 4 Review Vocabulary
Dilations

Use the definition map to list qualities about the vocabulary word or phrase.
Sample answers are given.

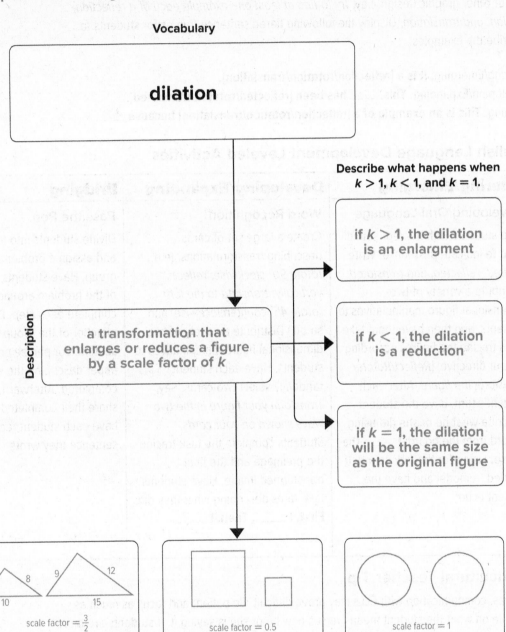

Vocabulary

dilation

Describe what happens when
$k > 1$, $k < 1$, and $k = 1$.

if $k > 1$, the dilation
is an enlargment

Description

a transformation that
enlarges or reduces a figure
by a scale factor of k

if $k < 1$, the dilation
is a reduction

if $k = 1$, the dilation
will be the same size
as the original figure

6 8
10
scale factor $= \frac{3}{2}$

9 12
15

scale factor $= 0.5$

scale factor $= 1$

Draw and label examples for $k > 1$, $k < 1$, and $k = 1$.

Lesson 1 Congruence and Transformations
English Learner Instructional Strategy

Sensory Support: Magazines and Newspapers

Divide students into small groups consisting of students with differing levels of English proficiency. Provide each group with a selection of magazines or newspapers. Direct students to search for examples of figures that have been rotated, reflected, or translated to create a logo or other graphic design. Say, *Try to find at least one example each of a reflection, rotation, and translation.* Display the following tiered sentence frames for students to describe the examples:

Entering/Emerging: **It is a [reflection/rotation/translation].**
Developing/Expanding: **This _____ has been [reflected/rotated/translated].**
Bridging: **This is an example of a [reflection/rotation/translation] because _____.**

English Language Development Leveled Activities

Entering/Emerging	Developing/Expanding	Bridging
Developing Oral Language Help students with the /ed/ sound used to indicate past tense. Write *rotated, reflected,* and *translated.* Distribute a variety of two-dimensional figure manipulatives to students, and then have them take turns tracing the figures according to your directive: [*Reflect/Rotate/Translate*] the figure. After each student's turn, have the student describe what he or she did using a word from the board: **I _____ the figure.** Listen for the /ed/ sound. If needed, remodel and have the student echo.	**Word Recognition** Create a large set of cards describing transformations. (e.g., *rotate 90° clockwise; reflect vertically; translate to the left; rotate 45° counterclockwise;* and so on.) Distribute a variety of two-dimensional figure manipulatives to students. Have each student randomly select two cards. Say, *Transform your figure in the two ways shown on your cards.* Students complete the task tracing the preimage and the final transformed image. Have students take turns describing what they did: **First, I _____. Then, I _____.**	**Pass the Pen** Divide students into four groups and assign a problem to each group. Have students pass a copy of the problem around the table to complete each step. Direct each member of the group to write a sentence or phrase on a strip of paper describing the step he or she completed. Afterward, have groups share their completed work, and have each student read the sentence they wrote.

Multicultural Teacher Tip

At times, communication with ELLs may prove difficult. Be patient and focus as much as possible on what the student means versus how he or she is saying it. If students are more comfortable with written versus verbal English, encourage them to write out solutions or steps leading to an answer. Allow students to use their native language if attempts at English are hindering their abilities to reason out the solution to a problem.

NAME _____ DATE _____ PERIOD _____

Lesson 1 Review Vocabulary
Congruence and Transformations

Use the definition map to list qualities about the vocabulary word or phrase.
Sample answers are given.

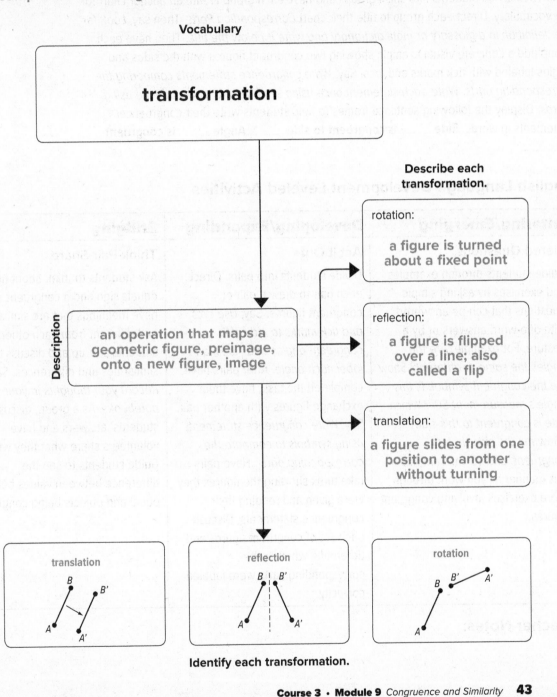

Vocabulary

transformation

Describe each transformation.

rotation:
a figure is turned about a fixed point

reflection:
a figure is flipped over a line; also called a flip

translation:
a figure slides from one position to another without turning

Description

an operation that maps a geometric figure, preimage, onto a new figure, image

translation

reflection

rotation

Identify each transformation.

Lesson 2 Congruence and Corresponding Parts

English Learner Instructional Strategy

Vocabulary Support: Anchor Charts

Write *corresponding parts* and its Spanish cognate, *partes correspondientes,* on the Word Wall. Then divide students into small groups and have each group create an anchor chart for the vocabulary. Direct each group to title their chart *Corresponding Parts.* Then say, *Look for the definition in a glossary or math dictionary and write it below the title.* Then have each group add a concrete visual example showing two congruent figures with the sides and angles labeled with tick marks and arcs. Say, *Write congruence statements comparing the corresponding parts. Write each statement once using symbols and a second time using words.* Display the following sentence frames to help students write their congruence statements in words: **Side _____ is congruent to side _____. Angle _____ is congruent to _____.**

English Language Development Leveled Activities

Entering/Emerging	Developing/Expanding	Bridging
Tiered Questions	**Act It Out**	**Think-Pair-Share**
Guide students through examples and exercises by asking simple questions that can be answered with one-word answers or by a gesture. For example, *Are the angles the same or different? Show me the congruent symbol. Is this angle's measurement 50°? Which side is congruent to this side? Show me the side that is congruent.* and so on. Continue in this manner as you work through more exercises involving congruent figures.	Divide students into pairs. Direct each pair to draw a pair of congruent figures. Say, *Use arcs and tick marks to indicate congruent angles and sides, and label each angle.* After pairs have completed the task, have them exchange figures with another pair. Say, *Write congruence statements using symbols to compare the corresponding parts.* Have pairs take turns showing the figures they were given and reading their congruence statements. Discuss each set of congruent figures and determine whether the corresponding parts were labeled correctly.	Ask students to think about how an equals sign and a congruent sign have meanings that are similar to and different from each other. Have students pair up and discuss the similarities and differences. Say, *Record your thoughts in your notebooks.* As a group, discuss students' answers and have volunteers share what they wrote. Guide students to see the difference between values being equal and objects being congruent.

Teacher Notes:

NAME _____ DATE _____ PERIOD _____

Lesson 2 Vocabulary
Congruence and Corresponding Parts

Use the word cards to define each vocabulary word or phrase and give an example. Sample answers are given.

Word Cards

congruent

Definition

if one image can be obtained by another by a sequence of rotations, reflections, or translations

Example Sentence

If a preimage is flipped, rotated, and/or translated, the image and the preimage are congruent. The corresponding parts of congruent figures are congruent.

congruente

Definición

si una imagen puede obtenerse de otra por una secuencia de rotaciones, reflexiones o traslaciones

---

Word Cards

corresponding parts

Definition

parts of congruent or similar figures that match

Example Sentence

The corresponding parts of congruent figures are congruent.

partes correspondientes

Definición

partes de figuras congruentes o semejantes que coinciden

Lesson 3 Similarity and Transformations

English Learner Instructional Strategy

Graphic Support: Graphic Organizers

Write *similar* and *scale factor* and their Spanish cognate, *similar* and *factor de escala,* on the Word Wall. To provide a concrete example for *similar,* compare two similar but not identical objects, such as a pair of pencils or different-colored connecting cubes. Then create a two-column chart labeled *Similar* and *Same,* and have students brainstorm examples that could go in each column. You might also include the English and Spanish spellings of *similar* in the *Same* column and the spellings of *scale* and *escala* in the *Similar* column.

For *scale factor,* have students look up the everyday meanings of each word. Use a Venn diagram to compare and discuss the everyday meanings with the math meanings. In the middle section of the diagram, record how the meanings are related.

English Language Development Leveled Activities

Entering/Emerging	Developing/Expanding	Bridging
Number Sense	**Show What You Know**	**Listen and Write**
Create a set of scale factor cards. Be sure to include values less than one, equal to one, and greater than one. Write *bigger, same, smaller.* As each student takes a turn drawing a card, say, *The scale factor is _____. Will the new figure be **bigger, the same,** or **smaller?*** Have the student answer, either by saying the word or by pointing to the correct word. If the student answers with a gesture, say the word and encourage him or her to echo. Continue until all students have had a turn.	Distribute a coordinate grid to pairs of students. Direct pairs to draw a triangle or quadrilateral in one of the quadrants. Then have them use a virtual three section (red, blue, and yellow) spinner to determine a scale factor for dilating their figure. Use the following values: $red = \frac{1}{2}$, *blue = 2, yellow = 3.* Have students draw the new figure, dilated by the determined scale factor and transformed one other way. Then have students describe the transformations using sentence frames: **The scale factor was _____. We also _____ the figure. The two figures are _____.** (similar)	Divide students into small groups. Say, *Listen and take notes. Then work together to answer the questions.* Read aloud the following problem: An art show offers different sizes of the same painting. The original print is 24 cm by 30 cm. A printer enlarges the original by a scale factor of 1.5 and then enlarges the second image by a scale factor of 3. What are the dimensions of the largest print? Are both of the enlarged prints similar to the original? Read slowly and enunciate clearly. Give groups time to complete the first question before asking the second one. Display sentence frames to help students share their answers: **The largest print is _____ centimeters by _____ centimeters. The enlarged prints are _____ because _____.**

Teacher Notes:

NAME _____ DATE _____ PERIOD _____

Lesson 3 Vocabulary
Similarity and Transformations

Use the definition map to list qualities about the vocabulary word or phrase.
Sample answers are given.

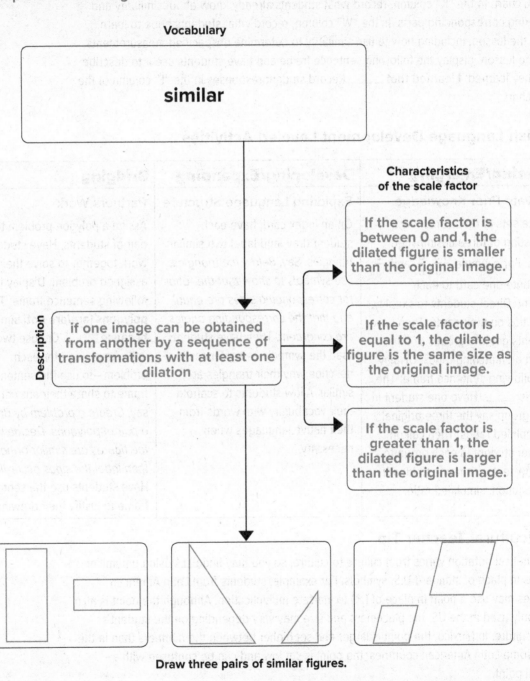

Vocabulary

similar

**Characteristics
of the scale factor**

If the scale factor is between 0 and 1, the dilated figure is smaller than the original image.

Description

if one image can be obtained from another by a sequence of transformations with at least one dilation

If the scale factor is equal to 1, the dilated figure is the same size as the original image.

If the scale factor is greater than 1, the dilated figure is larger than the original image.

Draw three pairs of similar figures.

Course 3 · Module 9 *Congruence and Similarity* **45**

Lesson 4 Similarity and Corresponding Parts
English Learner Instructional Strategy

Graphic Support: K-W-L Chart

Before beginning the lesson, display the following sentence frames: **A _____ has _____ sides. A _____ has _____ equal sides.** Have students use the sentence frames as you review vocabulary for two-dimensional shapes such as *quadrilateral, square,* and *rectangle.* Display a K-W-L chart. In the "K" column, record what students already know about similarity and comparing corresponding parts. In the "W" column, record what students hope to learn during the lesson, including how to use similarity to determine unspecified measurements. After the lesson, display the following sentence frame and have students use it to describe what they learned: **I learned that _____.** Record student responses in the "L" column of the K-W-L chart.

English Language Development Leveled Activities

Entering/Emerging	Developing/Expanding	Bridging
Activate Prior Knowledge	**Exploring Language Structure**	**Partners Work**
Create sets of ratio cards, each consisting of three unsimplified ratios. For example, $\frac{7.5}{10}$, $\frac{6}{8}$, and $\frac{12}{16}$. Distribute one card to each student. Direct students to simplify the ratios on their cards. Then have students get into groups of three based on matching ratios. Display the following sentence frame: **The ratio is _____.** Have one student in each group say the three original unsimplified ratios. Then call on another student in each group to use the sentence frame to identify the common, simplified ratio.	On an index card, have each student draw and label two similar triangles. Say, *Below the triangles, use symbols to show that the ratios for corresponding sides are equal and that the corresponding angles are congruent.* Then have students read the symbols as sentences to describe why their triangles are similar. Allow students to scaffold their vocabulary with words from their native languages when necessary.	Assign a polygon problem to each pair of students. Have students work together to solve their assigned problem. Display the following sentence frame: **The polygons [are/are not] similar because _____.** Choose two volunteers—one for each problem—to use the sentence frame to share their answers. Then say, *Create a problem by drawing a pair of polygons. Decide whether the figures are similar or not, and then label the sides accordingly.* Have students use the sentence frame to justify their drawings.

Multicultural Teacher Tip

Mathematical notation varies from culture to culture, so you may find ELLs using unfamiliar symbols in place of standard U.S. symbols. For example, students from Latin American countries may use a point in place of ($\times$) to indicate multiplication. Although the point is also commonly used in the US, the placement and size may vary depending on the student's native culture. In Mexico, the point is larger and set higher between the numbers than in the US. In some Latin American countries, the point is set low and can be confused with a decimal point.

NAME _____ DATE _____ PERIOD _____

Lesson 4 Vocabulary
Similarity and Corresponding Parts

Use the word cards to define each vocabulary word or phrase and give an example. Sample answers are given.

Word Cards

similar polygons	polígonos semejantes

Definition

polygons that have the same

shape

_____

Definición

polígonos con la misma

forma

_____

Example Sentence

The polygons are similar, so the

corresponding angles are congruent and the corresponding

sides are proportional.

Word Cards

scale factor	factor de escala

Definition

the ratio of the lengths of two

corresponding sides of two

similar polygons

Definición

la razón de las longitudes de

dos lados correspondientes

de dos polígonos

Example Sentence

The triangles shown have a scale factor of $\frac{3}{2}$.

---

46 **Course 3 · Module 9** *Congruence and Similarity*

Lesson 5 Indirect Measurement
English Learner Instructional Strategy

Sensory Support: Pictures and Photographs

Write *direct* and *indirect*. Underline the prefix *in-*, and say, *This word part means "not," so* **indirect** *means "not direct."* Have students brainstorm other examples of words that use the prefix *in-*, such as *incomplete, incorrect, informal, insecure, inaccurate.* Be sure to point out that not all words that start with *in-* use this meaning.

Create a two-column chart labeled *Direct* and *Indirect*. Show students photographs or illustrations of objects in a wide variety of sizes. For each object, ask students whether it would be measured directly or indirectly. Have students answer by saying **direct** or **indirect**. Tape up the photo or illustration in the corresponding column of the chart. Be sure students are saying the /ct/ sound at the end of each word. Some languages, including Spanish, do not commonly use consonant blends as final sounds, so the pronunciation may give students trouble. Model pronunciation as needed and have students chorally repeat.

English Language Development Leveled Activities

Entering/Emerging	Developing/Expanding	Bridging
Choral Responses	**Numbered Heads Together**	**Show What You Know**
Write *add* (+), *subtract* (−), *multiply* (×), *divide* (÷). As you work through examples, refer to the operations as you use them to solve the indirect measurement problems. As you say each term, have students chorally respond by repeating the word back to you. Continue in this manner as you model solving the following problem: *At the same time a 2-meter street sign casts a 3-meter shadow, a nearby telephone pole casts a 12.3-meter shadow. How tall is the telephone pole?* In addition, invite a volunteer to draw diagrams showing the sign, the pole, and their shadows. Direct the student to outline the similar triangles, and then use the ratios of corresponding sides to solve.	Organize students into groups of four and number off the students in each group as 1–4. Assign a problem to each group. Have the students in each group discuss the problem, agree on a solution, and ensure that everyone in the group understands and can give the answer. Afterward, call out a random number from 1 to 4. Have students assigned to that number raise their hands, and when called on, answer for their team.	Divide students into three groups, and give each group a sheet of drawing paper. Say, *Create your own indirect measurement problem. Use problems from the lesson as a guide.* After groups have completed the task, have them exchange papers and solve the problem they were given. Then have volunteers from each group describe the problem and how they solved for the unknown measurement.

Teacher Notes:

NAME _____ DATE _____ PERIOD _____

Lesson 5 Vocabulary

Indirect Measurement

Use the flow chart to solve a problem using indirect measurement.
Sample answers are given.

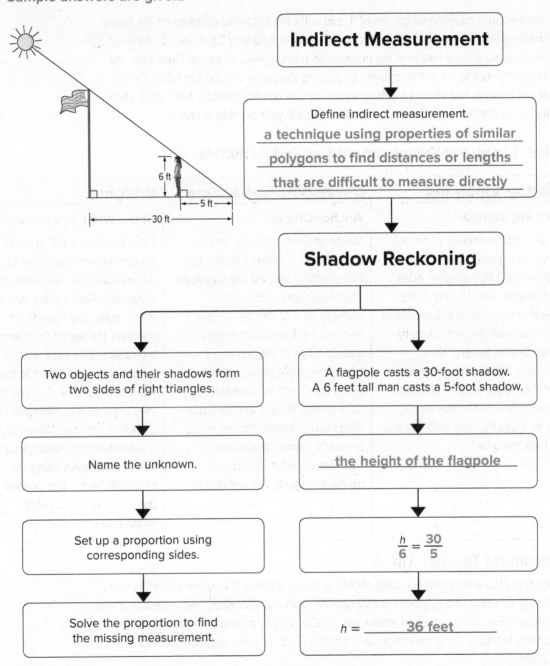

Indirect Measurement

Define indirect measurement.
<u>a technique using properties of similar</u>
<u>polygons to find distances or lengths</u>
<u>that are difficult to measure directly</u>

Shadow Reckoning

| Two objects and their shadows form two sides of right triangles. | A flagpole casts a 30-foot shadow. A 6 feet tall man casts a 5-foot shadow. |

| Name the unknown. | <u>the height of the flagpole</u> |

| Set up a proportion using corresponding sides. | $\dfrac{h}{6} = \dfrac{30}{5}$ |

| Solve the proportion to find the missing measurement. | $h = $ <u>36 feet</u> |

Lesson 1 Volume of Cylinders

English Learner Instructional Strategy

Collaborative Support: Round the Table

Write *volume* and *cylinder* and their Spanish cognates, *volumen* and *cilindro,* on the Word Wall. Briefly introduce the meaning of each word, and then, during the lesson, frequently refer to the Word Wall to reinforce meaning and to provide concrete examples for each term.

Place students into multilingual groups of 4, and write the following problem on the board: *To the nearest tenth, find the volume of a cylinder with a height of 1.8 in. and a radius of 3 in.* Have one student draw a model of the problem on a large piece of paper. Then have the other students work to solve the problem by passing the paper around the table. Each student will perform one step in a different color pen to find the volume. Afterward, choose one student to present the solution to the class. Repeat with another example.

English Language Development Leveled Activities

Entering/Emerging	Developing/Expanding	Bridging
Word Knowledge	**Anchor Charts**	**Show What You Know**
Use an empty container to model volume as capacity. Then fill the container with rice or some other small objects. Say, *Volume is the amount of space inside.* Say *volume* again and have students chorally repeat. Display several clear containers. Work with students to order them from least to greatest volume. Ask either/or questions, such as: *Does this one hold more or less than that one?*	Divide students into four groups. Say, *Choose a real-world example of something shaped like a cylinder. Then make an anchor chart showing how to find the volume of the cylinder.* Each chart should include a title at the top and a labeled example of the cylinder. When the charts are completed, have groups display and describe their charts. Display the following sentence frames for students to use: **Our cylinder is a(n) _____. [name of object] The volume is _____.**	Have students work in small groups. Have each group locate an example of a cylinder in the classroom. Give each group a metric ruler, and have them measure the object to determine the radius of its base and its height/length, rounded to the nearest millimeter. Say, *Use the measurements to determine the cylinder's volume.* Afterward, have a volunteer from each group share the measurement using the sentence frame: **The volume of the _____ is _____ cubic millimeters.**

Multicultural Teacher Tip

You may find ELLs write numbers using slightly different notations. In some countries, the groups may be separated by points (3.252.689) or spaces (3 252 689), and in Mexico it may be a combination of a comma and apostrophe (3'252,689) or a comma and semicolon (3;252,689). Similarly, some countries use a comma (3,45) to write decimals instead of a decimal point.

NAME _____ DATE _____ PERIOD _____

Lesson 1 Vocabulary
Volume of Cylinders

Use the vocabulary squares to write a definition, a sentence, and an example
for each vocabulary word. Sample answers are given.

volume	**Definition** the measure of the space occupied by a solid; standard measures are cubic units such as in^3 or ft^3
Example $V = Bh$	**Sentence** The volume of a cylinder is the area of the base multiplied by the height of the cylinder.

cylinder	**Definition** a three-dimensional figure with two parallel congruent circular bases connected by a curved surface
Draw a cylinder.	**Sentence** A real world example of a cylinder is a can of soup.

Lesson 2 Volume of Cones
English Learner Instructional Strategy

Vocabulary Support: Sentence Frames

Write *cone* and its Spanish cognate, *cono*, on the Word Wall. Provide a concrete example by displaying a cone manipulative or an example of a cone-shaped object in the classroom.

Display the following sentence frames to help students participate during the lesson:

Entering/Emerging: **The radius is _____. The height is _____. The volume is _____.**

Developing/Expanding: **If the diameter is _____, then the radius is _____. First we need to _____.**

Bridging: **I know the figure is a cone because _____.**

English Language Development Leveled Activities

Entering/Emerging	Developing/Expanding	Bridging
Academic Vocabulary	**Building Oral Language**	**Academic Word Knowledge**
Have students get into small groups and use translation tools to review any unknown vocabulary in the lesson. Have students write definitions for the terms in their notebooks and draw examples. Allow students to write the definitions in their own words and/ or in their native languages. Afterward, regroup students and have them share what they wrote with the students in the new group.	Divide students into pairs. Have each pair draw a model of a cone. Say, *Label the radius and height, and provide measurements for both.* Give pairs time to complete the task, and then have them exchange drawings with another pair. Say, *Find the volume of the cone.* Then write the formula for the volume of a cone: $V = \frac{1}{3}\pi r^2 h$. Have one student from each pair read the formula aloud using the measurements of the cone: **The volume is one-third times pi times _____ squared times _____. The volume is _____ square _____.**	Have each student draw a cone with the measurements of the radius and height labeled. Have students use the formula for finding the volume of a cone to determine the volume of the cone they drew. Several volunteers can verbally describe how they used the formula to find the volume. Gather students' drawings and put them together in a classroom portfolio that can be used for future reference or display them in the classroom.

Teacher Notes:

NAME _____ DATE _____ PERIOD _____

Lesson 2 Vocabulary
Volume of Cones

Use the word cards to define each vocabulary word or phrase and give an
example. Sample answers are given.

Word Cards

cone	cono
Definition	**Definición**
a three-dimensional figure with	una figura tridimensional con una
one circular base connected by	circular base conectada por una
a curved surface to a vertex	superficie curva para un vértice
Example Sentence	
Sometimes, a party hat is cone shaped.	

Word Cards

vertex	vértice
Definition	**Definición**
the point at the tip of a cone	el punto en la punta de un
	cono
Example Sentence	
Every cone has exactly one vertex.	

Lesson 3 Volume of Spheres
English Learner Instructional Strategy

Collaborative Support: Numbered Heads Together

Write *sphere* and *hemisphere* and their Spanish cognates, *esfera* and *hemisferio*, on the Word Wall. Provide concrete examples for *sphere* by locating spherical objects in the classroom or by having students brainstorm a list, such as *ball, globe, marble, bubble,* and so on. For *hemisphere,* identify the Northern and Southern Hemispheres on a globe and relate the geographical meaning to the math meaning.

Organize students into multilingual groups of four and number students as 1–4. Assign a problem to each group. They should discuss the problem, agree on a solution, and ensure that everyone in the group understands and can give the answer. Afterward, call out a random number from 1 to 4. Have students assigned to that number raise their hands and answer for their team.

English Language Development Leveled Activities

Entering/Emerging	Developing/Expanding	Bridging
Exploring Language Structure Write *sphere* and *hemisphere*. Underline the *ph* in each word. Slowly and clearly model pronunciation of each word, pointing to the *ph* as you say that word part. Write *ph = f* and provide some additional examples of words with *ph*, such as *graph, telephone, Phoenix, photo.* Say each word, emphasizing the /f/. Have students chorally repeat.	**Report Back** Write the following problem: *A ball has a diameter of 8 inches. It has a slow leak. Air is escaping at the rate of 2.5 cubic inches per second. How long would it take the ball to deflate? Round to the nearest tenth.* Have students work in pairs to solve. Display the following order words on the board: *first, second, then, next, last, finally.* Say, *As you solve, write a sentence describing each step. Use order words in your sentences.* After students complete the solution, have one student from each pair read the sentences they wrote. Provide a sentence frame for students to use when reporting the solution: **The ball would deflate in about _____ seconds.**	**Listen, Write, and Read** Have students get into small groups. Ask, *If you know the volume of a hemisphere, how would you find the volume of a sphere with an equal diameter?* Give groups time to discuss the question, and then have each student write a sentence or two describing the group's answer. Come together again as a single group, and say, *Exchange papers with another student.* Have students proofread for any errors in spelling, grammar, or punctuation, and then return the papers to their authors. Ask a few volunteers to read their answers.

Teacher Notes:

NAME _____ DATE _____ PERIOD _____

Lesson 3 Vocabulary
Volume of Spheres

Use the definition map to list qualities about the vocabulary word or phrase.
Sample answers are given.

Vocabulary

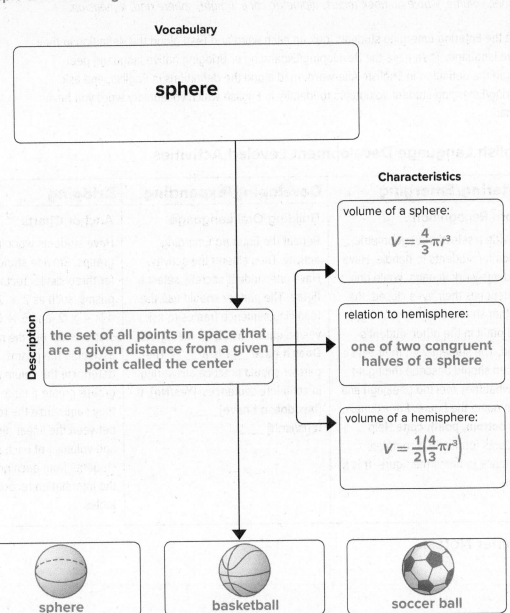

sphere

Characteristics

volume of a sphere:
$$V = \frac{4}{3}\pi r^3$$

relation to hemisphere:
one of two congruent halves of a sphere

volume of a hemisphere:
$$V = \frac{1}{2}\left(\frac{4}{3}\pi r^3\right)$$

Description
the set of all points in space that are a given distance from a given point called the center

sphere

basketball

soccer ball

Draw and label three examples of spheres.

Lesson 4 Find Missing Dimensions
English Learner Instructional Strategy

Collaborative Support: Native Language Peers

Before beginning the lesson, pair Entering/Emerging students with Developing/Expanding or Bridging students who share a native language. Direct them to use the multilingual eGlossary or other translation tools to review the following math vocabulary related to the lesson: *cylinder, volume, whole number, radius, diameter, cone, height, sphere and, dimension.*

Have the Entering/Emerging students look up each word and read aloud the definition in their native language. Then have the Developing/Expanding or Bridging native language peer provide the definition in English. Afterward, read aloud the definitions in English, and ask Entering/Emerging student volunteers to identify in English which vocabulary word you have defined.

English Language Development Leveled Activities

Entering/Emerging	Developing/Expanding	Bridging
Word Recognition	**Building Oral Language**	**Anchor Charts**
Provide a selection of geometric solids for students to handle. Have students work in pairs. While one student has their eyes closed, the partner should select a solid figure and put it in the other student's hand. The student with their eyes closed should describe the figure by what they feel (no peeking!) and then name the figure. For example, **flat bottom, point, cone** Help students formulate a complete sentence to name the figure. **It is a cone.**	Repeat the Entering/Emerging activity. Then extend the activity: Have one student secretly select a figure. The partner should use the following sentence frames to ask yes/no questions about the figure: **Does it have ___? Is it ___?** The partner should practice answering in complete sentences: **[Yes/No]**, it **[has/doesn't have]** ___. It **[is/isn't]** ___.	Have students work in small groups. Provide students with nets for three similar rectangular prisms, such as $2 \times 2 \times 1$, $4 \times 4 \times 2$, and $6 \times 6 \times 3$. Have students cut out the nets, assemble the prisms, and then determine the volumes. Have groups create a table in which they summarize the relationships between the linear dimensions, and volumes of each prism. Have students from each group share the information recorded in their tables.

Teacher Notes:

NAME _____ DATE _____ PERIOD _____

Lesson 4 Review Vocabulary
Find Missing Dimensions

Use the three-column chart to organize the vocabulary and key words in this lesson. Look at the figure. Write the word in English and Spanish. Then write the definition of each word.

	English	Spanish	Definition
	cone	cono	A three-dimensional figure with one circular __base__ base connected by a curved surface to a single __vertex__
	cylinder	cilindro	A three-dimensional figure with two parallel __congruent__ circular __bases__ connected by a curved surface
	hemisphere	hemisferio	One of two __congruent__ halves of a __sphere__
	sphere	esfera	The set of all points in space that are a given __distance__ from a given point called the __center__
	volume	volumen	The measure of the space occupied by a __solid__. Standard measures are __cubic__ units.

Lesson 5 Volume of Composite Solids
English Learner Instructional Strategy

Collaborative Support: Graffiti Poster

Ask students: *How can you find the **volume** of a three-dimensional composite figure?* Have students create a graffiti poster and list their ideas about their answer to the question. Have them include drawings and figures as well. Then have students turn and talk with a neighbor about their ideas. After students have had time to discuss, ask them to share with the class. As students share, make notes on the graffiti poster. Then tell students they will continue working with composite three-dimensional figures in this lesson. Make sure they add to the graffiti poster whenever they learn something interesting.

English Language Development Leveled Activities

Entering/Emerging	Developing/Expanding	Bridging
Look, Listen, and Identify Present models of several different composite figures to students. Point to each figure and ask, *How many three-dimensional figures are there?* Have students hold up an appropriate number of fingers. Then have them name the shapes that make up the composite figure. As language abilities allow, have students try completing the frame: **The composite figure is made up of ____.**	**Exploring Language Structure** Present models of several different composite figures to students. Have students identify the figures that make up each composite figure and then tell you the formula they would use to find the volume of each shape. To extend the activity, have students measure the faces of the figure. Then have them discuss each step for calculating its total volume with a partner. Finally, ask students to "coach" you through finding the total volume.	**Cooperative Learning** Organize students into three groups, and assign each group a problem involving three-dimensional composite figures. Have the students in each group work together to: 1) identify the figures used to form each composite figure; 2) decide how to calculate each figure's volume; and then 3) solve the problem. Once groups have completed their work, have each group present their problem to the other groups. Ask audience members to check the presenting group's calculations and make sure they agree the calculations are correct.

Teacher Notes:

Lesson 5 Notetaking
Volume of Composite Solids

Use Cornell notes to better understand the lesson's concepts. Complete each sentence by filling in the blanks with the correct word or phrase.

Questions	Notes
1. What is a composite solid?	A composite solid is made up of <u>more than one</u> three-dimensional solid.
2. How do I find the volume of a composite solid?	To find the volume of a composite solid, I must <u>decompose</u> the composite solid into separate three-dimensional solids. Step 1: Find the <u>volume</u> of each solid. Step 2: <u>Add</u> or <u>subtract</u> the volumes and <u>simplify</u>.

Summary

After you decompose a composite solid, how do you know if you should add or subtract the volumes of the individual figures? See students' work.

Lesson 1 Scatter Plots

English Learner Instructional Strategy

Vocabulary Support: Frontload Academic Vocabulary

Write *bivariate data* its Spanish cognate, *datos bivariantes,* on the Word Wall. Underline the prefix *bi-,* and say, *The prefix* bi- *means "two."* Help students brainstorm a few other examples of words with the same prefix, such as *bicycle, bifocal, biweekly.* Then circle -*variate* in the word. Ask students if this reminds them of any other words they know. Allow them a chance to answer, then write *vary, variation, variable.* Clarify that *bivariate data* is data that has two variables.

English Language Development Leveled Activities

Entering/Emerging	Developing/Expanding	Bridging
Memory Device	**Anchor Charts**	**Act It Out**
To help students understand *scatter plot,* arrange several manipulatives in a straight line. Say, *These objects make a line.* Then say, *I will* **scatter** *these objects.* Scatter several of the same type of manipulatives across the table. Then display a coordinate plane with a graph of a line alongside a graph with a scatter plot to provide a concrete example and reinforce meaning. Show two unlabeled scatter plots—one showing a positive relationship, and one showing a negative relationship. Above the charts write <u>p</u>ositive = <u>up</u> and <u>n</u>egative = dow<u>n</u>. Read each equation and have students repeat chorally.	Divide students into three groups, and distribute poster board, markers, and adhesive dots to each group. Then assign groups as *positive association, negative association,* and *no association.* Have each group use the materials to create a scatter plot demonstrating their assigned association. Have groups label each part of their completed model using math vocabulary, including a title that describes the type of scatter plot. Display students' work in the classroom, and encourage them to use it as a reference.	Divide students into three groups, numbered 1-3. Give each group a number cube, and direct groups to draw a graph with the *x*-axis labeled *number of turns* and ranging from 0–10. Have Group One keep a running total of what they roll and plot the increase. Have Group Two start at 100 and subtract what they roll each time, plotting the decreasing total. Have Group Three plot just each number they roll. Afterward, have groups identify the association demonstrated in their scatter plot: **Our scatter plot has ＿＿ association.**

Teacher Notes:

NAME _____ DATE _____ PERIOD _____

Lesson 1 Vocabulary
Scatter Plots

Use the word cards to define each vocabulary word or phrase and give an example. Sample answers are given.

Word Cards

bivariate data	datos bivariantes
Definition	**Definición**
data with two variables, or	datos con dos variables, o
pairs of numerical	pares de observaciones
observations	numéricas

Example Sentence

The data for the number of students in school for each day of

a week is bivariate data.

- -

Word Cards

scatter plot	diagram de dispersión
Definition	**Definición**
a graph that shows the relationship	gráfica que muestra la relación
between a data set with two	entre un conjunto de datos con dos
variables graphed on a coordinate	variables graficadas en un plano de
plane	coordenadas

Example Sentence

I can graph the points (day of the week, number of students in

school) as a scatter plot.

Course 3 · Module 11 *Scatter Plots and Two-Way Tables* **53**

Lesson 2 Draw Lines of Fit
English Learner Instructional Strategy

Sensory Support: Real-World Examples

Refer to the Word Wall to review math vocabulary relevant to the lesson (i.e. *scatter plot, positive/negative association, y-intercept, slope-intercept form*).

Display a K-W-L chart. In the first column, record what students already know about scatter plots and graphs, including the vocabulary reviewed before the lesson. In the second column, record what students hope to learn during the lesson, including how to make predications using lines of best fit. Have students use the following sentence frame to describe what they learned: **I learned _____.** Record student responses in the third column of the chart.

English Language Development Leveled Activities

Entering/Emerging	Developing/Expanding	Bridging
Making Connections	**Basic Vocabulary**	**Developing Oral Language**
Gather three hats. Be sure one is a "good fit" for you, either in style or size. Write *not good fit, good fit, better fit.* Start with a silly hat, or one that is much too big or small. Say, *This hat is not a good fit.* Then change into a hat that is a better fit, and say, *This hat is a good fit.* Put on the hat that best suits you, and say, *This hat is a better fit.* Then display a scatter plot and use a string to show options for lines of fit. Identify the line of fit, and have students chorally repeat **line of fit.**	Write 101 · 33 on the board. Ask, *I think the answer is 3300. Am I correct?* **no** Say, *My answer, 3300, is approximate. That means "nearly correct."* Repeat with other examples, such as guessing a student's age or height. Say *approximate* and have students repeat. Draw a simple scatter plot that shows how height changes with age, from age 2 through 12. Draw a line of fit. Point out that the *trend* is that children get taller each year. Have students use the scatter plot to predict how heights will change for four more years. Say *trend* and have students repeat. Then lead a discussion about how using line of fit can be an accurate predictor or not.	Have students work in small groups. Using a tape measure, have students measure each other's heights and keep a running total of the cumulative height of their group. Say, *Record the data in a table. Then use the data to create a scatter plot.* For example, the points (student number, cumulative height) of one scatter plot may be: (1, 63), (2, 122), (3, 175), and so on. Have each group draw a line of fit and use it to predict the cumulative height of ten students. Afterward, discuss how similar or different the groups' results are.

Teacher Notes:

NAME _____ DATE _____ PERIOD _____

Lesson 2 Vocabulary
Draw Lines of Fit

Use the definition map to list qualities about the vocabulary word or phrase.
Sample answers are given.

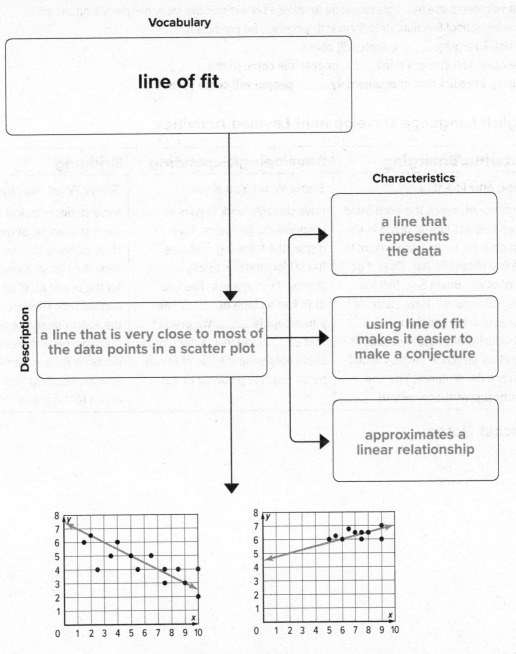

Vocabulary

line of fit

Characteristics

a line that represents the data

using line of fit makes it easier to make a conjecture

approximates a linear relationship

Description

a line that is very close to most of the data points in a scatter plot

Draw the lines of fit.

54   **Course 3 · Module 11** *Scatter Plots and Two-Way Tables*

Lesson 3 Equations for Line of Fit
English Learner Instructional Strategy

Language Structure Support: Explore Language Structure

During this lesson, students are asked to make conjectures. Write *conjecture* on the board. Tell students the word means "to predict using math evidence" or "a prediction." It can be a verb or a noun.

Have volunteers use available language to make a prediction how many people will attend an upcoming school function. Help them with language for predicting:

Entering/Emerging: _____ **people will come.**

Developing/Expanding: **I think** _____ **people will come to the** _____.

Bridging: **I predict that approximately** _____ **people will come to the** _____.

English Language Development Leveled Activities

Entering/Emerging	Developing/Expanding	Bridging
Look and Identify	**Show What You Know**	**Show What You Know**
Introduce or review the word *trend*. Have students look at graph in the first example in the lesson. Point to the line of best fit. Ask, *Does it go up or down?* **down** Say, *This line trends downward.* Have students repeat chorally and then individually. Have partners look at the other graphs in the lesson and practice the sentence, **The line trends [upward/downward].**	Have students work in pairs to complete the problems. Then display the following sentence frames for students to use in sharing their answers: **The line of fit has a slope of** _____. **The y-intercept is** _____. **We predict that** _____. Then lead a discussion about how using the line of fit can be an accurate predictor or not.	Have students look at the graph in the first example of the lesson. Have partners discuss what they think they know about the equation for the line of fit. What is the approximate y-intercept? What is the approximate slope? For each question, have students give evidence for their answer. Then have one student from each pair report to the group.

Teacher Notes:

NAME _____ DATE _____ PERIOD _____

Lesson 3 Vocabulary

Equations for Lines of Fit

Use the three-column chart to organize the vocabulary and key words in this lesson. Write the word in Spanish. Then write the definition of each word. Sample answers are given.

English	Spanish	Definition
line of fit	recta de ajuste	A line that is very close to most of the points on a <u>scatter plot</u>
scatter plot	diagrama de dispersión	A <u>graph</u> that shows the relationship between a data set with two variables graphed as <u>ordered pairs</u> on a coordinate plane
slope-intercept form	forma pendiente intersección	An equation written in the form $y = mx + b$, where m is the <u>slope</u> and b is the <u>y-intercept</u>
y-intercept	intersección y	The y-coordinate of the point where the <u>line</u> crosses the <u>y</u>-axis
slope	pendiente	The rate of change between any <u>two points</u> on a line. The ratio of the vertical change (<u>rise</u>) over the horizontal change (<u>run</u>).

Lesson 4 Two-Way Tables
English Learner Instructional Strategy

Graphic Support: Graffiti Poster

Write *relative frequency* and its Spanish cognate, *frecuencia relativa,* on the Word Wall. Briefly introduce the meaning and provide concrete examples for each term.

Before students begin the Independent Practice portion of the lesson, have them create a graffiti poster. Using colorful markers and large poster paper, write: *Two-Way Tables.* Have students help you brainstorm a topic for a survey, for example males versus females who like a certain food or type of music. Use the data to create a two-way table, and then have students interpret the results in writing on the chart. Also include definitions of any math vocabulary on the chart.

English Language Development Leveled Activities

Entering/Emerging	Developing/Expanding	Bridging
Tiered Questions	**Round the Table**	**Partners Work**
As you work through lesson examples, ask simple questions that can be answered with one-word answers or by a gesture. For example, *Do we multiply or divide to find a ratio? Show me the number we divide by. Which number shows _____? Which is the highest frequency ratio?* and so on. Continue in this manner as you work through the Extra Examples.	Divide students into three groups and assign each group a two-way table problem. Have the students in each group work jointly on the problem. Direct each member of the group to write with a different color pen or pencil to ensure all students participate. Afterward, have each group share their interpretations of the relative frequencies. Ask each student in the group to describe the specific steps he or she completed.	Divide students into pairs. Say, *Think up a survey you could conduct. Create an example of a two-way table using made up data of 100 people's responses to your survey.* Suggest ideas if necessary, such as cats/dogs/both/neither or paper/plastic/either/bring their own bags. Direct pairs to complete the task by drawing the tables in their notebooks, along with interpretations of the relative frequencies of the answers. Ask a few volunteers to share what they wrote.

Teacher Notes:

NAME _____ DATE _____ PERIOD _____

Lesson 4 Vocabulary

Two-Way Tables

Use the word cards to define each vocabulary word or phrase and give an example. Sample answers are given.

Word Cards

relative frequency

Definition

the ratio of the number of

successes to the total number

of attempts in an experiment

Example Sentence

The relative frequency of the number of students in the eighth grade

that play an instrument to all of the students in the school is $\frac{67}{158}$.

frecuencia relativa

Definición

razón del número de éxitos

experimentales al número total

de intentos experimentales

Word Cards

two-way table

Definition

a table that shows data that

pertain to two different

categories

Example Sentence

The two-way table shows that students that play an

instrument usually take art classes.

table de doble entrada

Definición

una tabla que muestra datos

que pertenecen a dos

categorías diferentes

Lesson 5 Associations in Two-Way Tables
English Learner Instructional Strategy

Collaborative Support: Act It Out

Survey the class. Have all students with long hair stand on one side of the room and all students with short hair on the other side. Gesture toward the "long hair" group and ask, *What do we notice about the group with long hair?* Students might note that most of the students with long hair are girls. Repeat for the "short hair" group. Say, *There may be an association between gender and length of hair.* Write association and say the word again. Have students repeat.

Repeat the activity for other, even more obvious things, to illustrate *no association* (e.g., wearing shoes today), *strong association* (likes to text message friends), or *weak association* (prefers dogs to cats).

English Language Development Leveled Activities

Entering/Emerging	Developing/Expanding	Bridging
Developing Oral Language	**Report Back**	**Communication Guides**
As you are going through the lesson with the class, be sure to check in with your Entering/ Emerging students to allow them to express their understanding in English, either in single words or short phrases or by completing sentence frames for simple sentences. For example, for this lesson, have them practice the frame, **There is [no/a strong/a weak] association.**	When reviewing an example or problem from the lesson, use the following frames to ask questions. *What is the relative frequency for ____?* (Repeat for each category in the two-way table.) Is there an association? For each question you ask, allow a bit of time for partners to deliberate and formulate their answers so they can report back to the group when called upon. **The relative frequency for ____ is ____. [Yes/No], there [is/is not] an association. The association is [strong/weak].**	Students have learned how to identify associations in two-way tables using relative frequencies. When they are working on review or test preparation, have students work together to describe the associations and the evidence that supports their claims. Suggest frames such as **There is [no/a strong/a weak] association because ____. The relative frequencies of ____ and ____ are ____, so that means the association is ____.**

Teacher Notes:

NAME _____ DATE _____ PERIOD _____

Lesson 5 Vocabulary
Associations in Two-Way Tables

Use the definition map to list qualities about the vocabulary word or phrase.
Sample answers are given.

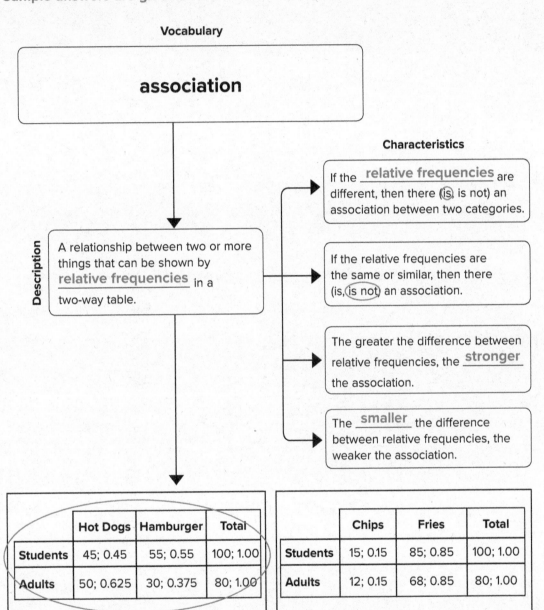

Vocabulary

association

Description

A relationship between two or more things that can be shown by **relative frequencies** in a two-way table.

Characteristics

If the ___relative frequencies___ are different, then there (is, is not) an association between two categories.

If the relative frequencies are the same or similar, then there (is, is not) an association.

The greater the difference between relative frequencies, the ___stronger___ the association.

The ___smaller___ the difference between relative frequencies, the weaker the association.

	Hot Dogs	Hamburger	Total
Students	45; 0.45	55; 0.55	100; 1.00
Adults	50; 0.625	30; 0.375	80; 1.00

	Chips	Fries	Total
Students	15; 0.15	85; 0.85	100; 1.00
Adults	12; 0.15	68; 0.85	80; 1.00

Circle the table that suggests an association between the categories.

Course 3 · Module 11 *Scatter Plots and Two-Way Tables* **57**

Dinah Zike Explaining
Visual Kinesthetic Vocabulary®, or VKVs®

What are VKVs and who needs them?

" VKVs are flashcards that animate words by kinesthetically focusing on their structure, use, and meaning. VKVs are beneficial not only to students learning the specialized vocabulary of a content area, but also to students learning the vocabulary of a second language. "

Dinah Zike | Educational Consultant

Dinah-Might Activities, Inc. – San Antonio, Texas

Why did you invent VKVs?

" Twenty years ago, I began designing flashcards that would accomplish the same thing with academic vocabulary and cognates that Foldables® do with general information, concepts, and ideas—make them a visual, kinesthetic, and memorable experience. "

I had three goals in mind:

- **Making two-dimensional flashcards three-dimensional**

- **Designing flashcards that allow one or more parts of a word or phrase to be manipulated and changed to form numerous terms based upon a commonality**

- **Using one sheet or strip of paper to make purposefully shaped flashcards that were neither glued nor stapled, but could be folded to the same height, making them easy to stack and store**

Why are VKVs important in today's classroom?

" At the beginning of this century, research and reports indicated the importance of vocabulary to overall academic achievement. This research resulted in a more comprehensive teaching of academic vocabulary and a focus on the use of cognates to help students learn a second language. Teachers know the importance of using a variety of strategies to teach vocabulary to a diverse population of students. VKVs function as one of those strategies. "

An Interview with

Dinah Zike Explaining
Visual Kinesthetic Vocabulary®, or VKVs®

Dinah Zike's
Visual
Kinesthetic
Vocabulary

How are VKVs used to teach content vocabulary to EL students?

" VKVs can be used to show the similarities between cognates in Spanish and English. For example, by folding and unfolding specially designed VKVs, students can experience English terms in one color and Spanish in a second color on the same flashcard while noting the similarities in their roots. "

What organization and usage hints would you give teachers using VKVs?

" Cut off the flap of a 6" x 9" envelope and slightly widen the envelope's opening by cutting away a shallow V or half circle on one side only. Glue the non-cut side of the envelope into the front or back of student notebooks or journals. VKVs can be stored in this pocket.

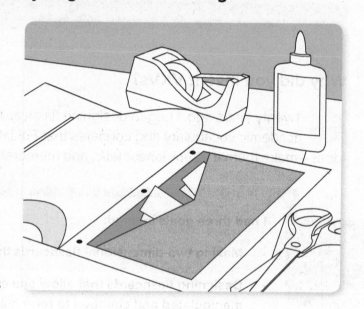

Encourage students to individualize their flashcards by writing notes, sketching diagrams, recording examples, forming plurals (radius: radii or radiuses), and noting when the math terms presented are homophones (sine/sign) or contain root words or combining forms (kilo-, milli-, tri-).

As students make and use the flashcards included in this text, they will learn how to design their own VKVs. Provide time for students to design, create, and share their flashcards with classmates. "

Dinah Zike's book Foldables, Notebook Foldables, & VKVs for Spelling and Vocabulary 4th-12th won a Teachers' Choice Award in 2011 for "instructional value, ease of use, quality, and innovation"; it has become a popular methods resource for teaching and learning vocabulary.

Dinah Zike's
Visual
Kinesthetic
Vocabulary

 cut on all dashed lines

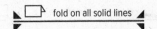 fold on all solid lines

Define exponent. (Define exponente.)

_____

_____

_____

exponente

b^x

base

Define base. (Define base.)

_____

_____

_____

racional

Circle the irrational number.

Spanish Translation

$\frac{5}{8}$ −6.5   12%

$\sqrt{8}$ 0.2222....

irrational number

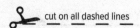
exponent
x

Rewrite as a power. (Reescribe como potencia.)

$6 \times 6 \times 6 \times 6 \times 6 =$ _____

The base is (La base es) _____ .

The exponent is (El exponente es) _____ .

número irracionales

rational

A rational number can be expressed as (un número racional se puede expresar como)

_____

base
b

Dinah Zike's
VKV
Visual
Kinesthetic
Vocabulary

✂ cut on all dashed lines   ⬜ fold on all solid lines

Write about a time when you would use scientific notation. (Escribe sobre una situación en la cual usarías la notación científica.)

Circle the perfect cubes. (Encierra en un círculo los cubos perfectos.)

6   9   27

125   200   625

Circle the radical sign. (Encierra en un círculo el signo radical.)

$\sqrt{}$ +

$\sqrt{}$ ×

scientific notation

perfect cube

radical sign

Circle the numbers written in scientific notation. (Encierra en un círculo los números escritos en notación científica.)

0.034 2.75×10^5

3×10^{-4} 98.3

Find each cube root. (Halla la raíz cúbica.)

$\sqrt[3]{-27} =$ _____

$\sqrt[3]{216} =$ _____

$\sqrt[3]{8,000} =$ _____

Simplify the expression. (Simplifica la expresión.)

$\sqrt[3]{216} =$ _____

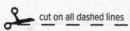 cut on all dashed lines

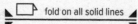 fold on all solid lines

radical

perfecto

científica

A radical sign is used to (El signo radical se usa para)

1,728 is a perfect cube. Explain why. (1,728 es cubo perfecto. Explica por qué.)

Write 8.64 × 10⁴ in standard form. (Escribe 8.64 × 10⁴ en forma estándar.)

Write 263,000 in scientific notation. (Escribe 263,000 en notación científica.)

signo

cubo

notación

Copyright © McGraw-Hill Education.

VKV6 **Visual Kinesthetic Learning**

Circle the multiplicative inverse of $\frac{5}{9}$. (Encierra en un círculo el inverso multiplicativo de $\frac{5}{9}$.)

$\frac{5}{9}$ $\frac{10}{18}$

$\frac{18}{10}$ $\frac{9}{5}$

Circle the identity. (Encierra en un círculo la identidad.)

$\frac{3}{4} - 12y = y + 1$

$12p + 6 = 6 + 12p$

$12x = 60$

$9s = 24 + s$

Definition/Definición

multiplicative inverse

identity

coefficient

Solve the equation using the multiplicative inverse. (Utiliza el inverso multiplicativo para resolver la ecuación.)

$\frac{3}{4}x = 2\frac{5}{8}$

Dinah Zike's Visual Kinesthetic Vocabulary

cut on all dashed lines

fold on all solid lines

multiplicativo

dad

e

inverso

The product of a number and its multiplicative inverse is (El producto de un número y su inverso multiplicativo es)

_____ .

An identity is an equation that is (Una identidad es una ecuación que es)

_____ .

What is the opposite of an identity? (¿Que es lo contrario de una identidad?)

_____ .

Circle the coefficients. Then solve the equations. (Encierra en un círculo los coeficientes y resuelve las ecuacións.)

$6x = 19.2$

$x =$ _____

$25 = \left(\frac{5}{8}\right)y$

$y =$ _____

$3\frac{1}{2} = 14m$

$m =$ _____

$5.4p = 48.6$

$p =$ _____

VKV8   Visual Kinesthetic Learning

Dinah Zike's
Visual
Kinesthetic
Vocabulary

cut on all dashed lines

fold on all solid lines

Define linear relationship.
(Define relación lineal.)

linear relationship

What does a linear relationship look like when it is graphed? (¿Cómo se ve la gráfica de una relación lineal?)

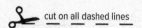

lineal

Write about a time when you might need to determine if a relationship is linear. (Escribe sobre una situación en la necesitarías determinar si una relación es lineal.)

relación

Dinah Zike's
Visual
Kinesthetic
Vocabulary

cut on all dashed lines

fold on all solid lines

Define substitution. (Define sustitución.)

substitution

system of equations

sistema de ecuaciones

stitución

Solve the system of equations. (Resuelve el sistema de ecuaciones.)

$y = 2x - 7$
$y = 5 - 4x$

(____ , ____)

Use substitution to solve the system of equations. (Resuelve el sistema de ecuaciones mediante el método de sustitución.)

$y = 3x$
$y = 5x - 6$

(____ , ____)

Define system of equations. (Define sistema de ecuaciones.)

_____
_____
_____

Dinah Zike's
Visual
Kinesthetic
Vocabulary

VKV

cut on all dashed lines

fold on all solid lines

Define relation. (Define relación.)

Define range. (Define rango.)

Define domain. (Define dominio.)

relation

range

domain

Dinah Zike's
Visual Kinesthetic Vocabulary

✂ cut on all dashed lines   📄 fold on all solid lines

inio

o

ción

State the domain of the relation below. (Calcula el dominio de la siguiente relación.)

{(−5, 4), (−7, 3), (−12, 11), (−14, 13)}

[   ]

State the range of the relation below. (Calcula el rango de la siguiente relación.)

{(6, −2), (8, 0), (12, 2), (18, 6)}

[   ]

Find four ordered pairs for the relation y = x + 4. (Enumera cuatro pares ordenados de la relación y = x + 4.)

(,   )
(,   )
(,   )
(,   )

VKV14   Visual Kinesthetic Learning

Dinah Zike's
Visual
Kinesthetic
Vocabulary

cut on all dashed lines

fold on all solid lines

Draw an example of a quadratic function below. (Dibuja un ejemplo de una función cuadrática.)

Write about a time when a qualitative graph might be useful. (Escribe sobre una situación en la que una gráfica de datos cualitativos sería útil.)

quadratic function

qualitative graph

Given an equation of a function, how can you tell if it is a quadratic function without graphing it? (Dada la ecuación de una función, ¿cómo puedes saber si es cuadrática sin necesidad de graficarla?)

Define qualitative graph. (Define gráfica cualitativa.)

Dinah Zike's
**Visual
Kinesthetic
Vocabulary**

✂ cut on all dashed lines   ◻ fold on all solid lines

cuadrática

cualitativa

Why is $y = x^2 + 5$ a quadratic function, while $y = x^3 - 9$ is not? (¿Por qué la función $y = x^3 - 9$ no lo es?
función $y = x^2 + 5$ es cuadrática y la

Circle the qualitative graph. (Encierra en un círculo la gráfica de datos cualitativos.)

A

Miles Driven

100
90
80
70
60
50
40
30
20
10
0

(1, 19)
(2, 38)
(4, 76)

0 1 2 3 4 5 6 7 8 9 10
Gallons Used

B

Height

Time

función

gráfica

VKV16   Visual Kinesthetic Learning

Dinah Zike's
**Visual
Kinesthetic
Vocabulary**

✂ cut on all dashed lines

fold on all solid lines

nonlinear function

lineal

Draw an example of a nonlinear function on the graph at the right. (Dibuja un ejemplo de una función no lineal en la gráfica de la derecha.)

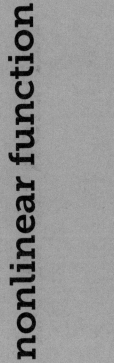

Dinah Zike's
V K V
Visual
Kinesthetic
Vocabulary

✂ cut on all dashed lines   ▱ fold on all solid lines

función no lineal

linear

Draw an example of a linear function on the graph at the right. (Dibuja un ejemplo de una función lineal en la gráfica de la derecha.)

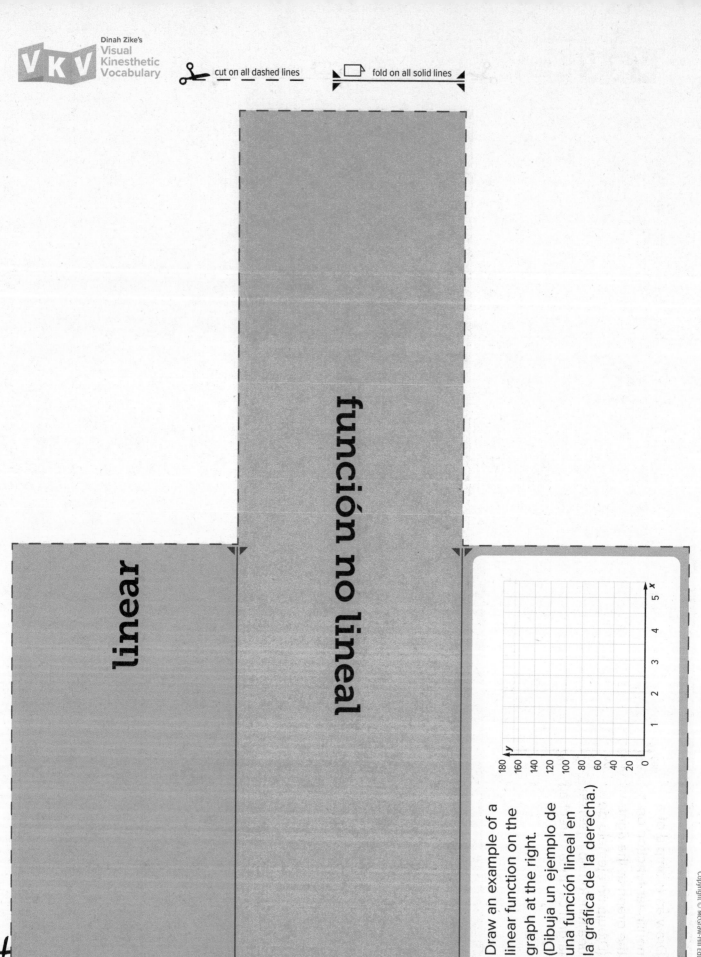

✂ cut on all dashed lines   ▱ fold on all solid lines

hypotenuse

The hypotenuse is the side opposite the (La hipotenusa es el lado opuesto al)

_____

_____

a

Circle the hypotenuse. (Encierra en un círculo la hipotenusa.)

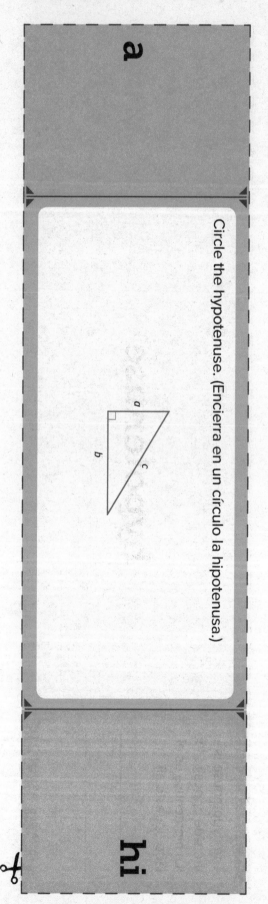

hi

Dinah Zike's
Visual
Kinesthetic
Vocabulary

✂ cut on all dashed lines

⬜ fold on all solid lines

Pythagorean Theorem

Write the Pythagorean Theorem. (Escribe el teorema de Pitágoras.)

$$\underline{} + \underline{} = \underline{}$$

Dinah Zike's
Visual
Kinesthetic
Vocabulary

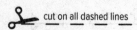
cut on all dashed lines

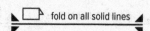
fold on all solid lines

Teorema de Pitágoras

Use the Pythagorean Theorem to find c. (Calcula c con ayuda del teorema de Pitágoras.)

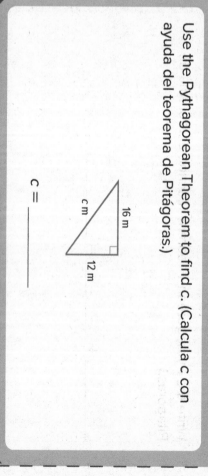

16 m

c m

12 m

c = _____

Dinah Zike's
VKV Visual Kinesthetic Vocabulary

✂ cut on all dashed lines

fold on all solid lines

Use the figure below to complete the following equation. (Completa la ecuación con ayuda de la siguiente figura.)

$$m\angle 6 = m\angle \underline{\qquad} + m\angle \underline{\qquad}$$

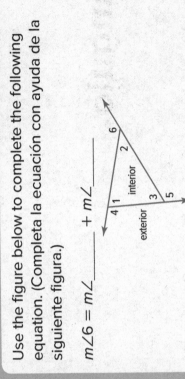

triangle

Draw an example of a regular polygon. (Dibuja un ejemplo de un polígono regular.)

regular polygon

Dinah Zike's
**Visual
Kinesthetic
Vocabulary**

✂ cut on all dashed lines   ▭ fold on all solid lines

ángulo

polígono regular

Define polygon. (Define polígono.)

A triangle has _____ vertices and _____ interior angles. The sum of the interior angles is _____°. (Un triángulo tiene _____ vértices y _____ ángulos internos. La suma de la medida de los ángulos internos es _____°.)

Define preimage. (Define preimagen.)

Define translation. (Define traslación.)

In which transformation(s) is the image congruent to the preimage? (¿En cuál(es) tipo(s) de transformación(es) la imagen es congruente con la preimagen?)

preimage

translation

congruent

Define image. (Define imagen.)

Dinah Zike's
Visual
Kinesthetic
Vocabulary
VKV

✂ cut on all dashed lines

📷 fold on all solid lines

e

slación

n

Triangle ABC is reflected over the x-axis. Label the image and the preimage. (El triángulo ABC se refleja sobre el eje x. Señala la imagen y la preimagen.)

Circle the graph with congruent triangles. (Encierra en un círculo la gráfica que representa triángulos congruentes.)

Circle the graph that demonstrates a translation. (Encierra en un círculo la gráfica que representa una traslación.)

pre

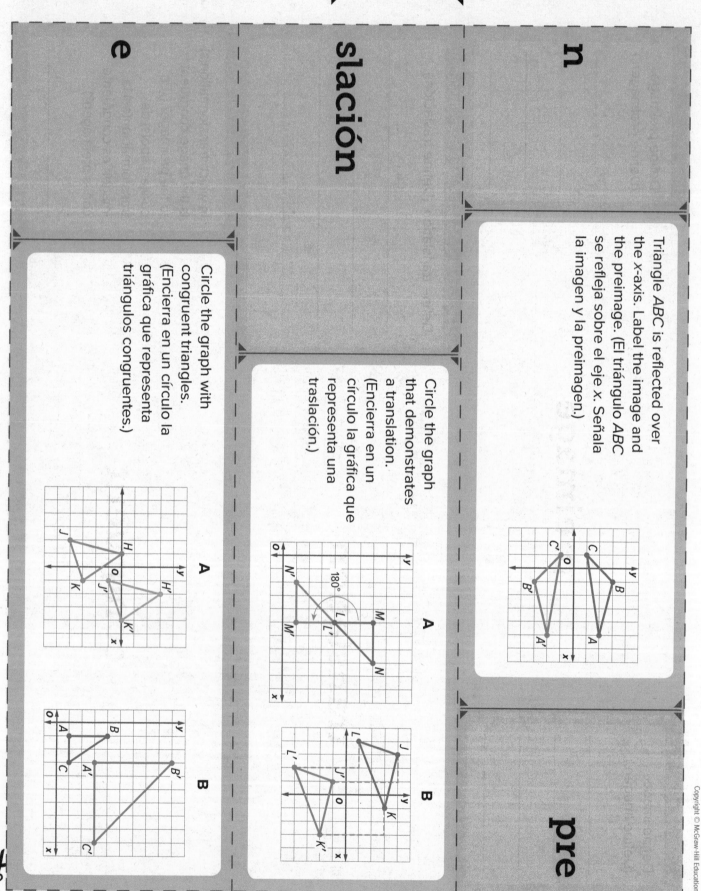

Dinah Zike's
V K V
Visual
Kinesthetic
Vocabulary

✂ cut on all dashed lines   fold on all solid lines

Define transformation.
(Define transformación.)

_____
_____
_____
_____

transformation

Identify the line of reflection. (Identifica el línea de reflexión.)

_____

line of reflection

Dinah Zike's
**Visual
Kinesthetic
Vocabulary**

✂ cut on all dashed lines

✄ fold on all solid lines

ción

línea de reflexión

Describe the transformation
shown in each figure.
(Describe la transformación
que se muestra en cada figura.)

A

B

Circle the correct phrase to complete the sentence below.

*In a reflection, the image is (congruent, not congruent)
to the preimage.*

(Encierra en un círculo la frase que completa
correctamente la siguiente oración.

*En un reflexión, la imagen (es congruente, no es
congruente) con la preimagen.)*

Dinah Zike's Visual Kinesthetic Vocabulary

cut on all dashed lines

fold on all solid lines

ángulo de

center of rotation

Circle the center of rotation. (Encierra en un círculo el centro de rotación.)

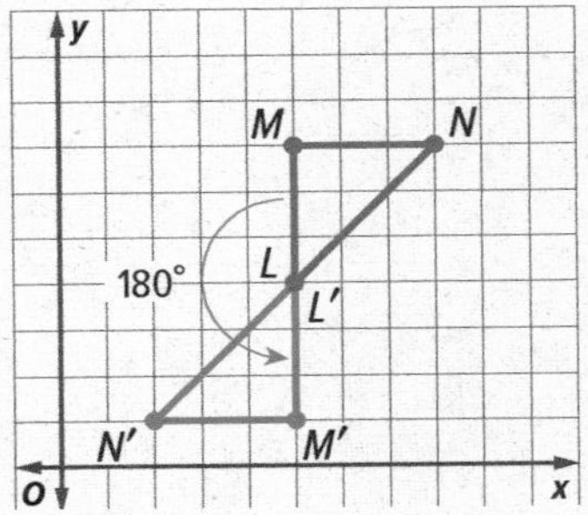

centro de rotación

angle of

Find the angle of rotation. (Calcula el ángulo de rotación.)

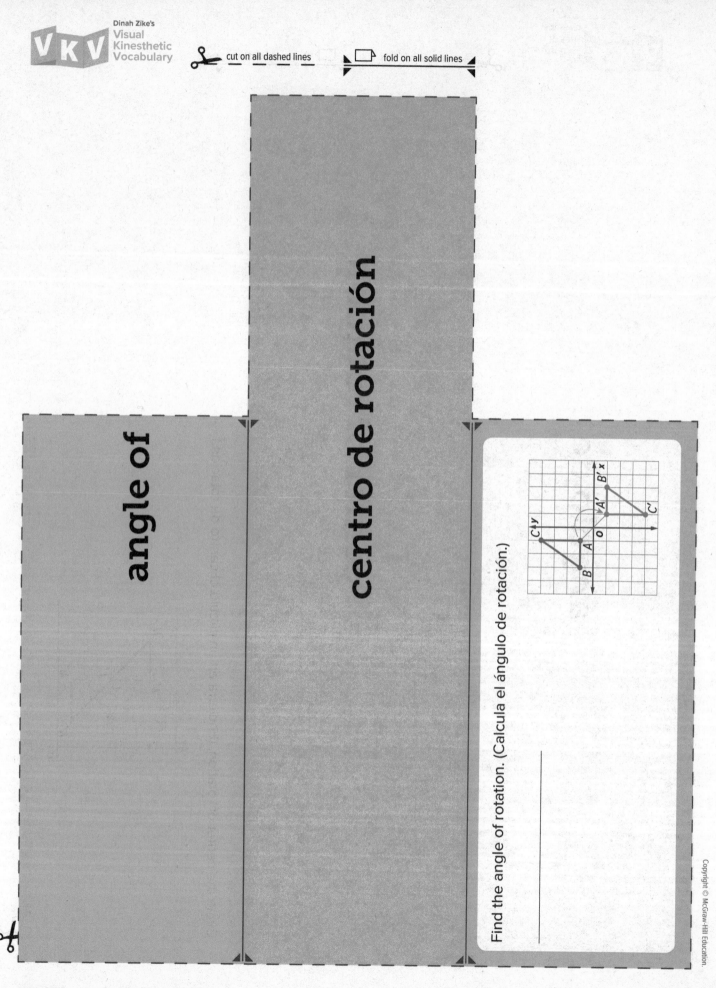

_____

Dinah Zike's
Visual
Kinesthetic
Vocabulary

cut on all dashed lines

fold on all solid lines

Encierra en un círculo la frase que completa correctamente la siguiente oración.

Si el factor de escala es menor que 1, la imagen es (más grande, más pequeña) que la preimagen.

¿Cómo puedes demostrar que en dos figuras congruentes los lados correspondientes son congruentes?

scale factor

corresponding parts

Circle the correct phrase to complete the sentence below.

If the scale factor is less than 1, the image is (an enlargement, a reduction) of the preimage.

In two congruent figures, how do you show that the corresponding sides are congruent?

Dinah Zike's
VKV
Visual
Kinesthetic
Vocabulary

✂ cut on all dashed lines   ⬚ fold on all solid lines

escala

correspondientes

Triangles *ABC* and *DEF* are similar. If $BC = 8$ cm, $EF = 2$ cm, and $CA = 12$ cm, what is *FD*? (Los triángulos *ABC* y *DEF* son semejantes. Si $BC = 8$ cm, $EF = 2$ cm y $CA = 12$ cm, ¿cuánto mide *FD*?)

$FD = $ _____

Triangles *ABC* and *DEF* are congruent. Name two pairs of corresponding parts. (Los triángulos *ABC* y *DEF* son congruentes. Menciona dos pares de partes correspondientes.)

factor de

partes

Dinah Zike's
Visual Kinesthetic Vocabulary

✂ cut on all dashed lines   ⬒ fold on all solid lines

Define cylinder. (Define cilindro.)

Define cone. (Define cono.)

cylinder

cone

✂ cut on all dashed lines

▢ fold on all solid lines

O

ilindro

Draw and label a net of the cylinder shown. (Dibuja el desarrollo del cilindro que se muestra. Señala sus partes.)

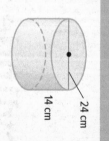

24 cm

14 cm

The formula for the volume of a cone is $V = \frac{1}{3}\pi r^2 h$. Find the volume of the cone shown. Round to the nearest tenth. (La fórmula para calcular el volumen de un cono es $V = \frac{1}{3}\pi r^2 h$. Calcula el volumen del cono que se muestra. Redondo a la décima más cercana.)

V = _____

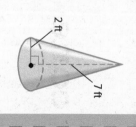

2 ft

7 ft

✂ cut on all dashed lines   ▭ fold on all solid lines

Define sphere.
(Define esfera.)

To the nearest tenth find the volume of the hemisphere. (A la décima más cercana calcular el volumen de la semiesfera.)

8 mm

$V =$ _____

sphere

To the nearest tenth find the volume of the sphere. (A la décima más cercana calcular el volumen de la esfera.)

9 in.

$V =$ _____

hemisphere

Dinah Zike's
Visual
Kinesthetic
Vocabulary

✂ cut on all dashed lines   ▭ fold on all solid lines

a

ferio

List three examples of real-world objects that are spheres.
(Menciona tres ejemplos de objetos reales que sean esferas.)

_____
_____
_____

The formula for the volume of a sphere is $V = \frac{4}{3}\pi r^3$. What is the formula for the volume of a hemisphere? (La fórmula para calcular el volumen de una esfera es $V = \frac{4}{3}\pi r^3$. ¿Cuál es la fórmula para calcular el volumen de una semiesfera?)

$V = $ _____

esf

Define symmetric. (Define simétrico.)

Define standard deviation. (Define desviación estándar.)

La frecuencia relativa de personas que tienen dos gatos con respecto a las personas que tienen al menos un gato es 0.83. Hay _____ personas con al menos un gato que tienen otro.

symmetric

standard deviation

relative frequency

The relative frequency of people who own two cats compared to those who have at least one cat is 0.83. _____ people with at least one cat have two.

Dinah Zike's
Visual Kinesthetic Vocabulary

✂ cut on all dashed lines

◄ ► fold on all solid lines

relativa

estándar

imétrico

Define relative frequency. (Define frecuencia relativa.)

Standard deviation relates to which measure: mode, median, mean, or range? (¿Con qué medida se relaciona la desviación estándar: moda, mediana, media o rango?)

On the number line, draw an example of a distribution that is symmetric. (Dibuja un ejemplo de distribución simétrica en la recta numérica.)

```
      0
 10
   20
     30
      40
       50
        60
         70
          80
           90
            100
```

frecuencia

desviación

Copyright © McGraw-Hill Education.

Dinah Zike's
Visual
Kinesthetic
Vocabulary
VKV

✂ cut on all dashed lines

▱ fold on all solid lines

Circle the correct word to complete the sentence.

Comparing the numbers of pools built in different months is an example of (univariate, bivariate) data.

(Encierra en un círculo la palabra que completa correctamente la oración.

Comparar la cantidad de piscinas construidas en distintos meses del año es un ejemplo de análisis de datos (univariados, bivariados.)

bivariate data

univariante

Dinah Zike's
**Visual
Kinesthetic
Vocabulary**

cut on all dashed lines

fold on all solid lines

datos bivariantes

univariate

Circle the correct word to complete the sentence.

The numbers of chicks hatched by twelve different chickens is an example of (univariate, bivariate) data.

(Encierra en un círculo la palabra que completa correctamente la oración.

La cantidad de pollos incubados por doce gallinas distintas es un ejemplo de datos (univariados, bivariados.)

VKV Answer Appendix

VKV3

exponente/base: See students' work for definitions.

irrational number: $\sqrt{8}$

VKV4

exponent/base: 6^5; 6; 5

rational: a fraction

VKV5

scientific notation: 2.75×10^5; 3×10^{-4}; See students' work.

perfect cube: −3; 6; 20; 27; 125

radical sign: 6; $\sqrt{}$

VKV6

cientifica notación: 2.63×10^5; 86,400

perfecto cubo: See students' work.

radical signo: indicate a positive square root

VKV7

multiplicative inverse: $\frac{7}{2}$; $\frac{9}{5}$ or $\frac{18}{10}$

identity: $12p + 6 = 6 + 12p$

coefficient: See students' work for definition.

VKV8

inverso multiplicativo: 1

identidad: true for every value of the variable

coeficiente: 6; $x = 3.2$; $\frac{5}{8}$; $y = 40$; 14; $m = \frac{1}{4}$; 5.4; $p = 9$

VKV9

linear relationship: See students' work for both exercises.

VKV10

lineal relación: Sample answer: a straight line

VKV11

substitution: See students' work.

VKV12

sustitución: (3, 9)

system of equations: See students' work; (2, −3)

VKV13

domain: See students' work.

range: See students' work.

relation: See students' work.

VKV14

dominio: −5, −7, −12, −14

rango: −2, 0, 2, 6

relación: (0, 4); (1, 5); (2, 6); (3, 7)

VKV15

quadratic function: Sample answer: If the equation has x^2 as the largest power in it, then it is quadratic; See students' work for drawing.

qualitative graph: See students' work for both exercises.

VKV16

función cuadrática: Sample answer: a quadratic function must contain an x^2. The function $y = x^3 - 9$ has a 3 as its largest exponent.

gráfica cualitativa: B

VKV17

nonlinear function: See students' work for drawing.

VKV18

función no lineal: See students' work for drawing. Chapter 5

VKV19

hypotenuse: right angle

VKV20

hipotenusa: See students work.

VKV21

Pythagorean Theorem: $a^2 + b^2 = c^2$

VKV22

Teorema de Pitágoras: 20 m

VKV23

regular polygon: See students' work for drawing.

triangle: 1; 3

VKV24

polígono: See students' work.
triángulo: 3; 3; 180

VKV25

congruent: translation, rotation, and reflection
preimage: See students' work for both exercises.
translation: See students' work.

VKV26

congruente: A
preimagen: See students' work.
translación: B

VKV27

line of reflection: y-axis
transformation: See students' work.

VKV28

linea de reflexión: congruent
transformación: A: rotation; B: translation

VKV29

center of rotation: See students' work.

VKV30

angelo de rotación: 180°

VKV31

corresponding parts: Sample answer: an equal number of tick marks is drawn on the corresponding sides.
scale factor: a reduction

VKV32

partes corresponientes: Sample answer:
$\angle A \cong \angle D$; $\overline{CA} \cong \overline{FD}$
factor de escala: 3

VKV33

cone: See students' work.
cylinder: See students' work.

VKV34

cono: 29.3 ft^3
cilindro: See students' work.

VKV35

hemisphere: 1071.8 mm^3
sphere: 3,053.6 in^3; See students' work.

VKV36

hemisferio: $V = \frac{2}{3}\pi r^3$
esfera: Sample answer: basketball, globe, orange

VKV37

relative frequency: More
standard deviation: See students' work.
symmetric: See students' work.

VKV38

frecuencia relativa: See students' work.
desviación estándar: mean
simétrico: See students' work.

VKV39

bivariate data: bivariate

VKV40

datos bivariantes: univariate